Mythology for Kids

Explore Timeless Tales, Characters, History, & Legendary Stories from Around the World. Norse, Celtic, Roman, Greek, Egypt & Many More.

History Brought Alive

© Copyright 2021 - All rights reserved.

The content contained within this book may not be reproduced, duplicated or transmitted without direct written permission from the author or the publisher.

Under no circumstances will any blame or legal responsibility be held against the publisher, or author, for any damages, reparation, or monetary loss due to the information contained within this book, either directly or indirectly.

Legal Notice:

This book is copyright protected. It is only for personal use. You cannot amend, distribute, sell, use, quote or paraphrase any part, or the content within this book, without the consent of the author or publisher.

Disclaimer Notice:

Please note the information contained within this document is for educational and entertainment purposes only. All effort has been executed to present accurate, up to date, reliable, complete information. No warranties of any kind are declared or implied. Readers acknowledge that the author is not engaged in the rendering of legal, financial, medical or professional advice. The content within this book has been derived from various sources. Please consult a licensed professional before attempting any techniques outlined in this book.

By reading this document, the reader agrees that under no circumstances is the author responsible for any losses, direct or indirect, that are incurred as a result of the use of the information contained within this document, including, but not limited to, errors, omissions, or inaccuracies.

Greetings!

As fellow passionate readers of history and mythology we aim to create the very best books for our readers.

We invite you to join our VIP list so that you can be the first to receive new books and exclusives. Plus you will receive a free gift!

Sign Up Today

https://www.subscribepage.com/hba

Table of Contents

Introduction 1
    History Brought Alive 3
        Citations 3

Chapter 1: What Are Myths? 4
    Types of Myths 7
        The Gods 7
        The Creation of Humans 7
        Human Behavior and Emotions 8
        Heroes 9
    Where Do Myths Come From? 9

Chapter 2: Ancient Egypt 11
    Who Were the Ancient Egyptians? 11
    The Myths of Ancient Egypt 12
        Creation 12
        Ra's Real Name 14

Chapter 3: Ancient Greece 17
    Who Were the Ancient Greeks? 17
    The Myths of Ancient Greece 18
        The Creation of Humans 18
        Prometheus Steals Fire 19
        Pandora's Box 20

The Flood 21

The Trojan War 22

Chapter 4: Ancient Rome..29

The Origins of Rome 30

Rhea Silva and Mars.. 31

The Wolf and the Shepherd 32

Romulus and Remus 32

Escape from Prison 33

The Foundation of Rome 34

Chapter 5: The Influence of Greece and Rome 37

Mercury 38

Venus 44

Mars 48

Jupiter, Saturn, and Uranus 49

Neptune 52

Pluto 54

Chapter 6: The Norse Myths 61

The Norse Gods 62

Odin 62

Thor 67

Tyr...73

Chapter 7: The Celts 80

Celtic Heroes 81

Cú Chulainn 81

Fionn MacCumhaill... 88

Oisín..94
Conclusion 101
Acknowledgments 103
References 106

Introduction

Most people just skip the introduction, so if you're reading this, well, that's all right. There won't be any stories or myths in this bit, but maybe we'll get to know each other a little bit better. I'm not saying that you should skip it, but no one will tell you off if you do.

Still here? Good! Let me tell you a little bit about this book. Just like this is the introduction to the book, this book is an introduction to mythology. No one could ever write just one book about all the myths. There are way too many! But that's good because it means you will never run out of stories.

Hopefully, after you've read this book you'll put it down (or maybe read it again!) and think—I WANT TO READ MORE! I know I would because myths are the greatest stories that anyone has ever written. Imagine, for thousands of years people have been telling each other stories. If it's a boring story, they just forget it (a lot of boring stories have been forgotten over the years). But if it's a good story, they tell it again and again and again. And everyone they tell it to tells someone else who tells someone else. Eventually, someone might even decide it's such an AMAZING story that they should write it down. Those are the myths we have today!

Of course, that means there are a lot of myths and a lot of books about them. At the end of this book, we will give you a list of some really good ones so you can keep reading and discovering more myths (we're not going to tell you what they are just yet, though—we want you to read our book first!).

Who knows, maybe one day you will want to read the really serious, long stuff like *The Iliad* or Ovid's *Metamorphoses*. Maybe you'll even decide to be one of those crazily intelligent people who learn Ancient Greek and Latin and how to read the Egyptian hieroglyphs (I'll tell you more about those later). Then you'll be able to read loads of really, really old books in strange languages and discover myths we had forgotten about. Or maybe you'll discover that there was a mistake in one of the myths and it actually said the exact opposite to what we thought (it has happened!).

For now, though, this book is just an introduction. It's like a tasting menu. Have you ever been to a really expensive restaurant? Me neither, but I've seen them on TV and a tasting menu is where instead of giving you just one big plate of spaghetti they give you lots and lots and lots of little plates of really weird food. I think they just want to show off how good at cooking they are. I would prefer a big plate of spaghetti.

But sometimes you just can't choose between the spaghetti or the pizza so it's nice to have a little bit of both. Maybe a slice of pizza and a bite of spaghetti. But then, which kind of pizza do you want? Maybe pepperoni or margherita? Or something with pineapple on it? Or are you one of those crazy people who like chicken on their pizza?

Well, with this book you get to have a slice of everything—a slice of Ancient Egyptian, Ancient Greek, Roman, Norse, and Celtic. Maybe you'll get to the end and think, "You know what? I actually *like* chicken on pizza!"

Enjoy your meal.

I mean your book! Enjoy the BOOK!

But don't eat it. It will make you sick.

History Brought Alive

At History Brought Alive we have a passion for everything from the past. The books we write are full of fun facts and even more fun stories that will make you think about the past and our ancestors in new and exciting ways. While we hope you will go on to read many more books about the subjects in ours—that is why we are writing them in the first place!—our books are ones you will return to throughout your life for information and entertainment.

Citations

Sometimes you might see a name and a date at the end of a sentence like this (Achilles, 2021). This means that someone else said the thing you have just read. It is important to give people *credit* for their work. Giving someone credit means saying, "I thought what you said was so good that I want to copy it, but I don't want people to think I said it first, so I will tell them that you did!"

This also means that if you want to know more about what that person said, you can go to the end of this book where there is a list of books and websites. This will tell you where the person said it. Then you can get their book or go to their website and read what they actually said!

Chapter 1: What Are Myths?

Have you ever thought about where you come from? You are not the only one. People have been wondering about where they come from and why they exist ever since they were able to think. No one knows how long ago that was exactly, but it was definitely many, many thousands of years ago. It probably wasn't the first thing they thought. The first thing they thought was probably, "I'm hungry," or "Oh my God! There's a saber-toothed tiger—run!"

The thing is, they wouldn't have been able to think "Oh my God" because they had not thought about gods yet. That would only have happened once they had escaped from the saber-toothed tiger and were safely in their cave. They would have sat around the fire and now that they had time to relax, they could wonder about less serious things like where they came from, or where that round silver thing in the sky came from, or where that round yellow thing in the sky during the day came from.

A lot of the time, as we will see, they decided that everything came from the round yellow thing in the sky. I am of course talking about the sun, but you knew that. They decided that the sun was so big and hot and powerful that it must have created everything, including the Earth and including them. In other places, they decided that everything was created by the thing they were sitting on, the Earth. They decided it was their mother.

But that wasn't enough. Once they had decided where everything came from, they had to explain where all the things came from. Nowadays we use science to explain these things, but for a lot of human history we weren't very good at science—everything takes practice, after all. So instead of science, people used stories to explain the things they saw around them. They had to explain why there were storms and why thunder was loud and why it was raining and where the animals came from and why life was so difficult. It was a lot more difficult back then than it is for you and me.

So they invented stories. Clearly, if there was a storm then someone was angry, weren't they? That was obvious. Storms are loud and noisy, just like angry people. A lot of the time, they decided the angry person must be a god. The god was angry because of something the humans had done. So the humans prayed and told the god that they wouldn't do it again. But that meant that someone had to decide why the god was angry in the first place and what exactly it was the people should not do again. In some places, they decided that the god must be angry because someone had killed their own brother and that killing was wrong. They promised never to kill again. In other places, they decided the god was angry because not enough people had been killed so they decided to go to war and kill a lot more. Sometimes they decided they had to make sacrifices to make the god happy. A sacrifice is where you give up something important to show how much you love or fear your god. It might seem like a horrible and not very intelligent solution to stopping a storm to you, but people used to think it worked!

But that wasn't everybody. In a lot of places, they thought one god was boring and obviously, the god of that tree over there can't be the same as the one in that river or in the sky. For those people, it made more sense that the storm was two gods arguing and that the thunder and the lightning were the gods hitting each other.

You will have guessed by now that these myths used to be religions! People thought this was how the world worked. But religions don't just explain the world around us—they also give us rules to live by. Myths often use stories to show these rules, telling us stories where someone didn't follow them and the terrible consequences that happened. A lot of these rules were things like, "Do what your parents tell you or you'll be eaten," or "Obey the gods or they will make you go and live somewhere very hot for a very long time." This second one is a bit like being sent to your room for being naughty, but a lot worse. It also caused a lot of problems because people often couldn't agree on what the gods actually wanted or how to obey them.

Myths are stories, and people have always told each other stories. A lot of the time they were stories about things like brothers and sisters fighting. Maybe that sounds familiar to you—if you're anything like me and my brother, you fight together all the time! Other stories they told were about love, jealousy, sadness, or happiness. Anything a human could think or feel was turned into a story. I love stories, you love stories, I guess, or you wouldn't be reading this right now! Myths are stories from a time when people had no television or films or internet or even books. All people had back then was the smelly old man who came and told some stories by the fire if you gave him some food and a bed for the night! Maybe that doesn't sound as good as watching a film with popcorn and a drink, but just imagine how good the stories had to be for people to put up with that smelly old man! Of course, I might be a smelly old man but you will never know.

Types of Myths

We've already talked about the myths about the creation of the world but there are many others. Here are just a few more subjects that myths tell stories about.

The Gods

There would be no myths without the gods. These often represent parts of nature like the sea or rivers or forests. They sometimes represent other things like beauty or death or war. Whatever they represent, the gods are like a big family that is always arguing about silly little things. Unfortunately for humans, what is silly and little for them is very big and serious for us. Gods also have the added bonus of being immortal. This means that they can never really die. They can be mean or nice, beautiful or scary, peaceful or violent. Many of the gods are all of these things at different times! This does not make them a very happy family, but it definitely makes the myths about them very entertaining.

The Creation of Humans

Following the creation of the world and the birth of the gods, there is a period in which the gods have fun falling in and out of love with each other, arguing and fighting, and generally causing trouble. After a little while, though, one of them will often get bored and decide they need something new to entertain them. So they create humans. They make these humans similar to themselves, which seems silly afterward because they always end up scared that the humans are better than them and will one day take over the world (maybe they were right!). To stop this from happening they give the new humans some rules. They tell the humans that if they follow these rules everything will be great and they will always be happy. You and I know what rules are though—annoying! Even the gods thought rules were annoying, so why they thought people wouldn't is a great mystery.

I am sure you have broken some rules. Well, so did the early humans. They often broke the only rule they were told not to break exactly because they were told not to! It is like an itch you just have to scratch or a big red button that says "Do Not Push!" The itch will be scratched. The button will be pushed. The gods become angry and they punish the humans. These myths are an explanation for everything bad in the world. Of course, we all know that it was really the gods' fault. They knew we would break the rules.

Human Behavior and Emotions

Just as there is a myth to explain all the bad things in the world, there is often a myth for everything a person does. These often also explain where our words come from. Did you know that another word for selfish is *narcissistic*? We have this word because a very handsome man called Narcissus was cursed, so when saw his reflection in a pond he fell in love with himself! He thought he was so handsome that he couldn't stop staring at himself and stayed there, admiring his own reflection for so long that he turned into a flower.

An emotion that is explained by a myth is *fury*. This is another word for anger and comes from the name of the three sister gods called the Furies. People prayed to the sisters when they were angry and wanted an enemy punished.

Heroes

Another type of myth tells the story of a hero. Sometimes these are human heroes, sometimes they are demi-gods. Demi is an old word for half, so a demi-god, as you have probably guessed, is a half-god. This means their mother or father was a god but their other parent was mortal. A demi-god is stronger than a normal person, but they always have a weakness. Sometimes, the weakness is in their personality—maybe they get angry too easily. Other times the weakness is physical. Achilles was a demi-god. When he was little his mother dipped him in a magic river to make him invincible. If you are invincible it means that nobody can hurt you. Too bad for Achilles, his mother forgot to dip the part she was holding him by—his ankle! He went on to become a great warrior until he was shot with an arrow in his ankle and died. Now we use the phrase "Achilles heel" to name someone's weakness. Chocolate is my Achilles heel—give me some chocolate and I will do anything for you! We also call part of the back of our foot our Achilles tendon.

Where Do Myths Come From?

Everywhere! Every country has myths. Sometimes even different parts of the same country have their own myths and during different times people told different myths. An interesting fact is that sometimes countries on opposite sides of the world have very similar myths even though it is unlikely they ever spoke to each other. In this book, we will read myths from Egypt, Greece, Italy, Scandinavia, and Ireland but there are also great myths from China, Japan, India, Saudi Arabia, Nigeria, and every other country in the world! Myths are something that all people have in common because we all wonder about the same things. Sometimes we come up with different ideas—someone who lives by the sea will tell different stories than someone who lives next to a volcano—but it is surprising how often we come up with the same ideas. Myths are stories, and stories bring people together.

Chapter 2: Ancient Egypt

Who Were the Ancient Egyptians?

Ancient Egypt started so long ago that people aren't even sure when it started! But we can be sure that their myths are from more than 5,000 years ago. I don't know how old you are, but that's 148 times older than me! The point is, even if we don't know exactly how old Ancient Egypt was, we know it was definitely *very old*.

You probably know a little about Ancient Egypt already. Maybe you have seen the pyramids and their writing—the hieroglyphs. Hieroglyphs use little pictures instead of letters and are very beautiful and fun to read and write but also very difficult to translate! A lot of the myths we have from Ancient Egypt come from people reading the hieroglyphs they found inside the pyramids. The pyramids were where kings and queens were buried. I am sure you have heard of mummies as well, but do you know why the Ancient Egyptians wrapped themselves up in bandages like that? They did it for the same reason we put food in the fridge instead of leaving it out in the sun—so that it doesn't go bad! This was important to the Ancient Egyptians because they believed they would wake up again in the Afterlife, and they needed their body and all their things when they did. That's why the pyramids were full of treasure and artifacts; these objects tell us how the Egyptians lived when they were alive. Maybe they wrote the myths on the walls because they knew they would need something to read when they woke up as well—they were worried the Afterlife would be boring!

The Myths of Ancient Egypt

Creation

The Ancient Egyptian myth of creation starts with a sea of nothing which they called Nun. From this rose a pyramid, and from this pyramid the god, Atum, created himself. You might be thinking, "Well, that doesn't make much sense, how did he create himself?" This is a good question. Explaining the beginning is a problem all myths have. Even our modern science has a little difficulty with it.

Your teachers have probably told you that the beginning of everything was the Big Bang, but the greatest scientists in the world are still arguing about what happened before the Big Bang. Maybe when you are older you will become a scientist and find out the answer, but then someone will ask you, "What happened before the thing that happened before the Big Bang?" Then, you will have to keep looking.

So you can see, this isn't just a problem the Ancient Egyptians had. Once Atum had created himself, things started to make a little more sense (but not much). Atum had a lot of names, but he is probably best known as Ra. Ra was the sun god. The fact that the Egyptians thought he came first is understandable because it is such a hot country and mostly desert.

Sitting on his pyramid with nothing to do and no one to talk to, Ra got bored and lonely. You and I know how boring things can be if there is nothing on television or our parents have told us not to use the computer, and even then we could read a book or go outside and play or visit our friends. Ra had none of this. He just had to sit there staring at the nothing all around his pyramid, probably wondering why he had wasted any time creating himself.

But Ra was a god, and gods can do whatever they want. Ra decided he would make some other gods so that he would have company. His way of doing it was a bit strange though—he spat and he sneezed. When he spat he created Tefnut, the god of moisture. When he sneezed he created Shu, the god of the air.

Now, I don't know about you, but to me that sounds a lot like *atishoo*! Think about it, you have a tickle in your nose and your head goes back and you go, "Tef-tef-tef- TEFNUTSHU!" and out of your nose and mouth come moisture and air. The only difference between when you and Ra sneeze is that he is a god, so when he sneezes the moisture and air that came out were gods like him. Crazy, right? But try not to think about the fact that everything in existence comes from Ra's boogers!

That was just the beginning. Tefnut and Shu then had two children: Geb and Nut. Geb was the Egyptian god of the earth, Nut was the Egyptian god of the sky. Geb and Nut had some kids as well. They were called Osiris, Horus the Elder, Isis, and Nephthys.

From these nine gods came everything else in the world, not to mention a lot of trouble!

Ra's Real Name

Something you are going to find out from reading this book is that gods are not the easiest people to get along with. The Ancient Egyptian gods were no exception. They were constantly fighting with each other for power, tricking each other, making and breaking agreements, and generally being difficult. Maybe this is because Ancient Egyptians thought of their gods as being like pharaohs. Pharaoh is another word for king. In fact, many Egyptian pharaohs became gods themselves. At least, they said they did. It's up to you whether you believe them or not. The pharaohs were always fighting for power, so it seemed only natural to the Egyptians that the gods were too.

One day, Isis decided that she wasn't powerful enough. She thought the best way to get power was to get control over Ra, her great grandad. He was the most powerful at the time, even though he was very old. If she had power over him, then she would have power over everything. The best way to get power over a person was to discover their real name. Now, when it comes to you and me it isn't too difficult to discover our real name. It's the one we use every day! Ra was different though. We already know he was also called Atum, but he had a lot of other names as well. This was because he was the creator of everything and had different names when he was doing different things. In some ways this makes sense. Think of one of your teachers for example. You might call them Mr. Jones or Ms. Jones. But their friends might call them Tom or Alice. Their husband or wife might call them love or sweetheart or darling (ew! I know!). Maybe they have kids, so their kids probably call them dad or mom. In the future, those kids might also have kids and they will call your teacher—Mr. or

Ms. Jones to you—grandad or granny. Which of those is their real name? It's hard to say, isn't it?

Isis had to discover Ra's real name. He wasn't stupid though—he knew the power that names had, and he wouldn't tell it to anyone. Isis had to find a way to trick him. She was clever, though, and she had a plan. She knew that if she got a bit of his body—some hair or skin or a toenail, for example— she could make a spell that would injure Ra very badly. As Ra was now very old, he drooled all over the place. We already know how powerful some of Ra's drool could be—he used it to create Tefnut and Shu! All Isis had to do was follow behind him and scoop his drool up off the floor. It was icky, but it was worth it. Once she had enough of his drool, she mixed it with some dirt to make clay and from the clay she made a giant snake. She nailed the snake to the ground (so it was already very angry!) on a path she knew Ra went down.

Poor Ra, old and weak, didn't know what was coming when he set off on his daily trip around Egypt to check that everyone was okay. He was the creator, after all, so he still had a lot of responsibility. Maybe because he was old, but his eyes and ears were getting so bad that he didn't see or hear the snake. Or maybe he had been that way so many times he wasn't being careful. Either way, the snake bit him and injected him with all its venom. Remember, this wasn't a normal snake. It had been made from Ra's own spit, so it was very strong and had powerful venom.

It was the most painful thing Ra had ever felt, and he had been around forever and had felt everything! He was in *agony*. He called to all the gods and everyone who knew magic and begged someone to make the pain go away. All of them tried, but no one could find the cure.

Then Isis came and said, "Oh, what's wrong, Grandad?" Like she didn't know. Ra explained that he had been bitten by a deadly snake and that he was in a lot of pain. Now Isis knew her plan was working and she said, "Well, the only way I can cure this type of snakebite is with the real name of the person who has been bitten."

Ra began to list all the names of the things he had created and done because these were also his names and he thought he could trick Isis into using one of these. But Isis shook her head, "No, it has to be your *real* name, otherwise there's nothing I can do."

By this time Ra had probably figured out what had happened, but it was too late. He tried to ignore the pain and refused to say his real name but he couldn't take it. "Fine!" he said, finally, "My real name is written on my heart. Here." And he gave his heart to Isis.

His great-granddaughter did as she had promised and performed the magic to cure the snakebite. It worked and he was cured, but now Isis had Ra's heart *and* his real name. This meant that she also had his power. So while Ra was no longer in agony, he was also no longer a god.

I would love to tell you what Ra's real name was. Maybe if we knew it *we* would have all the power of a Ra. But Isis wasn't about to share that secret with anyone. She was now the most powerful god in Egypt and she wanted it to stay that way.

Chapter 3: Ancient Greece

Who Were the Ancient Greeks?

The Ancient Greeks lived on the other side of the Mediterranean from the Ancient Egyptians. In fact, a very famous Greek soldier called Alexander the Great invaded Egypt more than 2,300 years ago and became a pharaoh (National Geographic Society, 2019). The Ancient Greeks are very famous for their philosophy and learning. Alexander the Great's teacher was one of the most famous philosophers ever: Aristotle. And, of course, they are famous for their myths. We know Alexander the Great knew the myths because he copied some of the things he had heard or read about in them (Encyclopedia Britannica, n.d.). He did this because he wanted people to think of him as one of the heroes from the myths. That way they would respect him more, and maybe be afraid of him.

This is another reason myths were important in the past. They were often used by rulers to connect themselves to heroes and gods from mythology. If they could make themselves seem like a hero in a myth it told people something about them. A ruler who was a soldier like Alexander wanted people to think of him as strong and powerful. Maybe he also wanted people to think of him as a demi-god.

The Myths of Ancient Greece

There are some similarities between the Ancient Greek and Ancient Egyptian myths. They both say that the world was created from nothing, but the Greeks called nothing *chaos*. This is a word we still use today to mean something is badly organized. To the Ancient Greeks, it meant emptiness. Another similarity is that the Ancient Greek gods were always fighting for power, just like the Ancient Egyptian ones. They had two different names for their gods, though: gods and Titans. Titans were actually gods as well.

In Ancient Greece, Zeus was the king of the gods. He had taken his throne on Mount Olympus from his father Cronus, one of the Titans. Zeus imprisoned Cronus and the rest of the Titans, apart from Prometheus and Epimetheus. He left these two free if they agreed to help him create men and all the animals and plants and things of the Earth that men would need to live.

Some of you reading this might be thinking, "What about women?" The fact is, Zeus decided he didn't want any women to be made because his wife, Hera, would be jealous (Fry, 2017). Hera's jealousy was completely understandable—Zeus was a terrible, terrible husband and could never be trusted.

The Creation of Humans

Why Zeus thought the world needed humans is a difficult question to answer. He had a lot of brothers and sisters, just as many wives and lovers, and even more children! It seems that wasn't enough for Zeus, though, who felt like something was missing. Some people think he was just bored (Fry, 2017).

Either way, he ordered Epimetheus to get to work and for Prometheus to keep an eye on him. They had to make all the animals and give them the tools they needed to survive—claws and wings to birds, teeth to tigers and lions, scales and the ability to breathe underwater to fish. Unfortunately, Epimetheus wasn't watching what he was doing and by the time he came to the men, there was nothing left to give them! So he had to ask his brother, Prometheus, for help (Bullfinch, 1885).

Prometheus made the men out of clay, but they had no way to survive. Prometheus felt bad for the men and decided there was one thing that would help them—fire. There was one problem, though. Zeus was scared of the men becoming too powerful! He'd asked for them to be made in the first place, yet now he was scared of them! And he knew that the one thing that would help them become more powerful was fire, so he told Prometheus that they could never have it.

Prometheus Steals Fire

But Prometheus wasn't one to follow the rules. He had also become very fond of his creation and didn't like to see them suffering as they were. He decided that he would steal the fire from the gods. The best place to get it, of course, was the sun. Obviously, only an idiot would try and chase down the sun while it was flying across the sky. It would be too hot and moving too fast. But during the night, it was a different matter. By then the sun had cooled down, like a fire that was about to go out.

So Prometheus crept into the cave where the sun was hidden, waiting for the next day, and stole a piece of it. He took it down to the men and showed them how to use it. Finally, they were able to make all the tools they needed to survive and to cook and warm their homes.

Pandora's Box

Of course, when Zeus found out that Prometheus had disobeyed him he was furious. Perhaps you remember the word "fury"? Well, furious is the word describing a person who is feeling very angry.

Furious, yes, but not out of control. A lot of gods might have started throwing thunderbolts and letting off volcanoes and flooding the world (he would do that later). Instead, he decided to set a kind of trap for the men. So he made the first woman. Her name was Pandora. He asked all the gods to give her something. Aphrodite gave her beauty, and Athena taught her how to sew which, to be honest, does not seem much of a gift. Some people said that other gods made her jealous and cruel and a liar, but that is just because those people were angry with Pandora for what she did. Her only real weakness was curiosity, which is not a weakness at all unless a god has tricked you. And Zeus definitely did trick her because before she went he gave her a gift: A box which he told her never to open.

I'm sure you know what it feels like to be carrying around something you can't open. Just think of what it's like the night before your birthday, or on Christmas Eve, when you know there are presents in the house! You know you will be able to open them the next day, and still it's difficult not to go and look, to peel back just a tiny bit of the wrapping paper and see what's inside. Imagine if you were given a present and told you could *never* open it! Do you think you could do it? I know I couldn't.

Pandora couldn't either. She managed for a while but her curiosity won in the end. She opened the lid of the box just a tiny bit, just for a peek, and out flew all the bad things in the world, things like illness and murder and hatred and disease and lies. As soon as she realized what was happening, Pandora shut the box again, trapping inside one last thing—hope.

People argue about whether this means we still have hope, kept safe in the box for all time, or if it is the opposite. If only she'd left the box open for another second, there would be hope in the world as well. You will have to decide which sounds correct yourself. I'm afraid I can't help you there.

The Flood

A giant flood happens in almost every mythology and religion in the world. There is one in Babylonian mythology, Arabic mythology, Ancient Egyptian mythology, as well as in Christianity and Judaism. These floods often happen because the god or gods of the place were said to be unhappy with the humans' behavior. Zeus was the only one who was angry at the human behavior he had *caused*. Imagine, all the trouble that humans were experiencing in the world, all the lying and the cheating and the stealing and the war was because of the box he had given to Pandora! And we all know that he knew she would open it. He created her and he knows, just like you and I know, that you can't ask someone not to open their present!

It doesn't seem fair, then, that he was angry about the bad things the humans were doing. We should be thankful that he didn't go with his original plan—to burn everything. That might have been worse. But the only reason he didn't do that was that he was scared the fire might reach Mount Olympus, where he and the other gods lived.

So he called on Poseidon, his brother and the god of the sea, to help him send a flood. Zeus himself made earthquakes and storms and between them, they washed away all of humanity. All apart from two—Pyrrha and her husband Deucalion. Zeus remembered that of all the people these two were the only ones who had worshipped him as much as he liked to be worshipped (which was a lot), so he sent away the storms and told Poseidon to relax and bring the oceans and rivers back down.

Zeus was happy again, although I'm not sure he deserved it. Poor Pyrrha and Deucalion had to start all over again. Humanity had to start all over again.

The Trojan War

Washing humanity off the face of the Earth wasn't a permanent solution. That's probably because the humans weren't really the ones causing the trouble. Yes, you guessed right, it was the gods. Zeus was what we call a hypocrite. This means someone who tells people they believe one thing but then does the exact opposite. Zeus being annoyed at humans for arguing and causing trouble was very hypocritical. The greatest war in Ancient Greek mythology, the Trojan War, was actually the gods' fault as much as it was the humans'. The Trojan War is probably the most famous of all the Greek myths. There is a whole book about it called *The Iliad* by someone called Homer.

The Golden Apple

The Trojan War started because someone wasn't invited to a wedding. That might sound like a silly reason to start a war, but a lot of wars start for silly reasons. In this case, it was Eris, the goddess of discord, who wasn't invited. Discord means not getting along or fighting or causing trouble. Perhaps that is why she wasn't invited to the wedding. No one wants arguments and trouble at their wedding. It made her very angry, though. Or maybe she started out very sad and lonely, but you and I know that our emotions can change when we think about them too long. Sometimes sad people act in very angry ways.

Have you ever not been invited to a wedding? Okay, maybe a wedding is a bad example. They're boring and it's better not to be invited! But have you ever not been invited to something like a birthday party? Everyone else is going but for some reason, the birthday girl or boy hasn't invited you. If that has happened to you, you know how bad a feeling it is to be left out. If that hasn't happened to you, you are very lucky.

It is not nice to be left out, and Eris was as sad about it as you or I would be. Being the goddess of discord, her solution to being left out was to cause trouble. She found a golden apple and wrote "For the most beautiful" on it. She then crept up to where the wedding was happening. Everyone was drinking and laughing and having fun (imagine how Eris must have felt hearing and seeing all of those people enjoying themselves without her!). She rolled the apple into the middle of the dancefloor and, as if by magic, there was discord. Who was the apple for? It said the most beautiful, but at least three of the wedding guests thought that meant them!

In an attempt to stop the arguing, the three most beautiful of the guests—Aphrodite, Hera, and Athena—went to Zeus. They wanted him to decide who was the most beautiful. Now, Zeus wasn't the most tactful god in history—if you are tactful that means you are good at talking to people without being rude or making people angry—but this time he knew he had to be careful. Hera was his wife, and Aphrodite and Athena were his daughters. He knew that if he chose one, the others would hate him. Of course, if he had been a good parent or husband, he might have done what parents have done throughout history and told them that they should share!

Instead, Zeus decided to avoid the question and said that the three goddesses should ask someone else. He even chose the person: A very handsome prince called Paris. Paris was from a city called Troy, which is where we get the name the Trojan War from. You might have guessed, then, that things are not going to go well for Paris.

Why Zeus thought Paris was a good choice to make this decision is a mystery. Knowing Zeus, he probably thought Paris was the worst person to decide the winner. But Zeus seemed to enjoy discord as much as Eris did.

Aphrodite, Hera, and Athena went to Paris and demanded that he tell them who was the most beautiful. You have to feel sorry for Paris in this situation. The gods are very scary. It doesn't matter if they are beautiful or not, they can still do terrible things to people, sometimes just for fun! So imagine you have to choose between three! It would be something like your parents coming and standing in front of you and asking who you think is best! You don't want to have to make that decision.

Poor Paris had no choice. I say poor Paris, but he probably managed to make the worst decision possible for the worst possible reasons. He accepted one of their bribes. Aphrodite promised him the most beautiful woman in the world, Helen, would be his wife if he chose her. Paris, the idiot, accepted her bribe. Aphrodite was declared the winner of the golden apple. Paris had Helen.

Helen

Now, there are several problems with this situation. The first is that we never really hear what Helen thought about this. No one asked her if she wanted to be with Paris. The second problem is that Helen was already married to a very powerful man, Menelaus. She had chosen Menelaus out of many men and was happy with him. To make matters even worse, all Menelaus' friends and supporters had promised to protect her.

Then, Paris turned up at Menelaus' house and was welcomed as a friend. Hospitality, being nice to people in your house, was very important to the Greeks. It was also important for the guest not to be rude to their host. There are not many things ruder than stealing someone's husband or wife. That is what Paris did. Some people say that he persuaded her to run away with him, but that seems a little strange. Why would she leave her husband to run away with someone she barely knew?

Whether he kidnapped her or she chose to run away with him, in the morning Paris and Helen were gone and Menelaus was very, very angry. Furious even. Nowadays, if someone is kidnapped, we would probably call the police. But in Ancient Greece there were no police. So Menelaus got all the people who had promised to protect Helen together and said they were going to war. They agreed, maybe because they felt bad because they had let her be kidnapped in the first place!

The Trojan Horse

The Trojan War lasted ten years. There was a lot of fighting, and a lot of people on the Greek and the Trojan sides died. But Troy was a big city with big walls and the Greeks never managed to break them. As long as the Trojans were safe behind those walls and the Greeks were outside, the war would never end.

A Greek king called Odysseus, one of Menelaus' friends, realized the war could go on forever this way. But Odysseus was famous for being very intelligent, and so he came up with a solution. You might wonder, if he was so smart, why didn't he come up with this solution ten years earlier? I don't know. He could have saved a lot of lives. But it was a very unusual solution, and over the ten years the Greeks tried all the normal ways of attacking a city. They tried climbing over the walls during the night—that didn't work. They tried knocking the walls down with big boulders—that didn't work. They even tried just hanging around until the Trojans ran out of food and water. You guessed it, that didn't work either.

Which maybe explains why Odysseus thought the best solution was to build a giant wooden horse. Even some of the other Greeks probably thought this was a bit weird. But they knew Odysseus was smart, so they did what he said and they built the horse.

One morning the Trojans woke up and went up to the walls, ready for another day of fighting. But when they looked out they saw that all the Greeks had taken their ships and left during the night! All that was left behind was a giant wooden horse. The Trojans were happier than they'd been in a long time. They had won the war! The Greeks had gotten tired and went home. Not only that, but they'd felt so bad about the whole thing that they had built this lovely wooden horse to say sorry. So the Trojans opened the gate and went out and pulled the wooden horse inside and had the biggest party they'd ever had. They probably drank too much alcohol, which is what adults do at parties. And as any adult will tell you, when you drink too much alcohol you will regret it the next day. They have probably never regretted it as much as the Trojans, though. They drank and they partied and they drank some more until eventually, they all fell into a deep sleep.

Maybe if they hadn't drunk so much they would have woken up when the second part of Odysseus' plan started. Because the Greeks didn't build the horse as a present. They built it as a trick. Inside the horse, hiding the whole time, was Odysseus and some other Greek soldiers. When they heard the party coming to an end and the snores of all the drunk Trojans, they opened a hidden trapdoor and climbed out of the horse. They then ran to all the gates and opened them. Outside, the Greek army was waiting. They had not run away, they had just been hiding out of sight. And while the Trojans were partying they came quietly back, ready for Odysseus to open the gates.

Troy was destroyed. Paris was dead. Menelaus was back with Helen. She had always loved him. She had even helped the Greeks during the war, so her husband knew she had been kidnapped and was happy to have her back. And we have Odysseus to thank for the phrase "a trojan horse", which we use when something disguised as something good turns out to be something very bad.

We also have Odysseus to thank for the word odyssey. If something is an odyssey it means it was a very long and difficult journey full of danger and excitement. We have this word because, while Menelaus and Helen were already back home playing happy family, it took Odysseus another ten difficult years to make it home!

That is nothing, though, if you think about the poor Trojans who no longer had a home to go to. But this was not the end of their story, as we will see.

Chapter 4: Ancient Rome

Ancient Rome and Ancient Greece had a lot of things in common. A lot of their culture is very similar and most of their gods were the same but with different names. This is because, even after they conquered Greece, the Romans still felt that Greek culture was better and they sent their children to study with the Greek philosophers.

But that didn't mean they thought the Greeks themselves were better. Obviously, the people who conquered the Greeks were better than the Greeks. Yes, they had culture, but if they were really better than the Romans, then they wouldn't have lost all the battles. That was how the Romans saw it.

In order to show this, the Romans used myths in a way that was a bit like how Alexander the Great used them. They told stories to show how they were superior to the Greeks. To do this, they actually used some of the Greek myths.

One thing they said was that when Zeus defeated his father Cronus, he didn't actually manage to imprison him. Instead, Cronus, who the Romans called Saturn, escaped and went to live with Janus. Janus was the god of Rome. He had two faces, one looking forwards and the other looking backward. The one looking forward represented the future, and the one looking backward represented the past (although, how you know which way is forwards or backward when you have two faces, I don't know). From his name, we get the word January.

The Romans worshipped all the other Greek gods as well but, as mentioned, they gave them different names. The gods weren't the only part of Greek mythology the Romans stole, though.

The Origins of Rome

We've already seen how myths were used to explain the beginning of the world and the beginning of people and the beginning of a war. The Romans also used myth to explain the beginning of their city. Maybe because Greece had such a powerful culture, the Romans wanted to be clear that they were different. Maybe you have a brother or sister who is very close to you in age. Do people say that you look the same, or that you could be twins? If that has happened to you, you will know how annoying it is! Or maybe you have an older sibling who you copy a lot. You think they are cool and you want to be like them (even if this annoys them!). Someday, you will decide you want to have your own identity and you will decide to dress very differently from them and listen to different music. But still, you will always know your older sibling taught you a lot of things.

The Romans were like the Greeks' younger siblings in that way. They had copied them for many years, but now that they were older and more powerful, they wanted the world to know that they were different. To do this, they took the story of the Trojan War and made a kind of sequel.

Some of the Trojans survived when their city was destroyed. One of them was called Aeneas. He was a cousin of Paris. When the Greeks came in and destroyed his city, he ran away to Italy and started a family. Some of his descendants—

his great, great, great-grandchildren—would be the founders of Rome. Their names were Romulus and Remus.

Rhea Silva and Mars

Romulus and Remus' family got along about as well as the Greek gods, which is to say not well at all. Their mother was called Rhea Silvia.

Rhea's father was a king called Numitor. He had a brother called Amulius. One day Amulius imprisoned Numitor and made himself king. But he was still scared of Numitor's children, especially the boys. He was afraid that they would come back when they were older and kill him for what he had done to their father. So he decided to kill them first. He didn't kill Rhea because she was a girl. This was pretty sexist of Amulius, but I'm sure Rhea didn't complain about that at the time. Instead, he made her become a nun. He did this because nuns were not allowed to marry, so she would never have children.

We've already seen what happens when someone tells a person they can't do something in myths. Rhea didn't marry anyone, to be fair to her, but one day she met a man walking in the woods. He had a woodpecker and a wolf with him, which is a hint that he wasn't a normal man. In fact, he wasn't a man at all. He was Mars, the Roman god of war.

Rhea and Mars fell in love and Rhea became pregnant. When Amulius heard about this, he used it as an excuse to throw Rhea in prison for breaking the rules. Then, when she gave birth to two boys, he ordered that they should be taken to the river and drowned.

The Wolf and the Shepherd

There is a saying that Amulius had obviously never heard: If you want something done right, do it yourself. The people he sent to drown the twin boys didn't do the job he had sent them to do. Instead, they just threw the boys and the basket they were in into the river. Eventually, the basket bumped against the bank and the babies fell out.

It was cold and they were wet and hungry so the babies did what babies do and they cried. A she-wolf heard them crying and came to them. Maybe it was the same wolf that had been with the boys' father, Mars, or maybe it was another one. Either way, the wolf looked after the boys, cleaning them and giving them milk to drink until a shepherd, Faustulus, found them.

Faustulus took the boys home and brought them up as his own children. He was pretty sure they were the children of Rhea. Everyone had heard what Amulius had done by then. Faustulus knew that they were safer with him. The two boys grew up not knowing who they were. They had a good life, even if they weren't rich. Shepherds are normally peaceful people who do not attack their brothers and kill their nephews so, in many ways, it was better than being a king.

Romulus and Remus

Romulus and Remus *were* kings, though. More than that, they were demi-gods. So while the life of a shepherd might have been nice, they got bored of it quickly. Instead of looking after the sheep, they ran around the countryside and played together and went hunting. Other boys thought the twins were very cool, and they followed them around in a gang. Soon enough, the twins thought hunting and running and playing was boring too and, together with their followers, they started robbing people. They were good boys, though, so they decided only to rob bad people. They decided to rob a gang of robbers!

Unfortunately for Romulus and Remus, these robbers were friends with King Amulius. This isn't surprising really. We already know Amulius was a bad guy, so it makes sense that he was friends with other bad guys. But it made the whole situation a lot more dangerous for Romulus and Remus.

The robbers soon found out where the twins lived. Romulus was able to escape, but the robbers caught Remus and took him to Amulius' prison. When Romulus ran home and told the shepherd what had happened, the old man was worried. If Amulius realized who Remus was, he would kill him! So he told Romulus that he and his brother were really princes.

Escape from Prison

Do you remember Numitor? He was Romulus and Remus' grandfather. For some reason, Amulius wasn't particularly scared of him. He had been scared of all the other boys in Numitor's family, so why wasn't he scared of Numitor? Numitor was the only one who could actually hurt him. The others were just babies! Perhaps Numitor was a coward. That is the only thing that explains why Amulius even let him out of prison and let him stay in the castle!

Romulus sent a message to his grandfather. The message said that Numitor had two grandsons and that one of them was in the castle's prison. Numitor was so surprised that he didn't believe the message at first. Maybe he thought it was his brother trying to trick him. To see if it was true, he went and looked at Remus in the prisons. Remus looked so much like Rhea that Numitor knew he was his grandson. He agreed to help them.

Numitor tricked Amulius into thinking that an army was coming to attack. Amulius sent his soldiers to fight the army. Once again, he made the mistake of not going himself. As soon as the army was gone, Romulus attacked the castle. He had all the shepherds and his and Remus' followers to help him. With no one to defend the castle, Amulius was helpless, and Romulus killed him. Maybe if Amulius hadn't been lazy and had gone with his army he could have come back and taken over the castle again. Fortunately for Romulus and Remus, he was lazy.

Numitor was made king again, although you have to wonder why. He had not shown many kingly qualities. But he was made king, and Romulus and Remus agreed to help him.

The Foundation of Rome

Romulus and Remus soon became bored again. Perhaps, just like the king part of them meant they weren't happy being shepherds, the shepherd part of them meant they weren't happy being kings! Either way, they decided they wanted to make their own city instead of helping their grandfather with his. If only they had been happy with what they had. That would have saved them a lot of trouble.

They went back to the hills where they had been shepherds and looked for a good place to put a city. By this time the twins had a lot of followers. They agreed to go with them to found the city. Some of them were the ones who had followed them when they were children. Others were probably people who thought, like us, that Nimutor wasn't a very good king and didn't want to hang around when the twins had gone!

So the two brothers wandered the hills with their followers, looking for the best place to build a city. Remus chose one hill and said it would be the best place. Romulus chose another. Some of the followers agreed with Remus. Some of them agreed with Romulus. The ones who agreed with Remus said *he* would be the founder. The ones who agreed with Romulus said that it would be *him*. In the end, they couldn't agree who was right, so each of them started building their own city.

Now, I don't know if you have any siblings, but if you do you know that sometimes things can become very competitive. If you see your sibling doing something, you want to do it bigger and better. Sometimes you might start trying to annoy your sibling, saying that your thing is better than theirs. This is how a lot of arguments start.

The argument between Romulus and Remus started like that, but it got out of control. One day Remus came over to see how Romulus's city was coming along. Romulus had started building his wall. He said it was going to be a great wall and that no one would be able to get through it. Remus laughed. The wall was still very low. He said it was a useless wall. "Look," said Remus, still laughing, "I can just jump over it!" And he did. He jumped one way and then the other, laughing all the time about how small Romulus's wall was.

"Stop it," said Romulus. "Shut up! It's obviously not finished. When it's finished you won't be able to jump over it!"

But Remus wouldn't shut up, and he wouldn't stop jumping over the wall and laughing. We all know what it's like when someone is being annoying. We try to control ourselves, we try to ignore them, but sometimes it just gets too much. Unfortunately for Remus, Romulus had a sword and when he got annoyed, he killed him.

He probably didn't mean to kill his brother. He probably just got angry. Sometimes when we are angry we don't think about what we are doing and bad things can happen. That is why our parents tell us that when we are angry we should count to ten. If Romulus had counted to ten, he probably wouldn't have killed his brother. But he didn't count to ten, so he had to live with that for the rest of his life.

He did build his city, though, and he called it Rome. Which makes you wonder how bad he actually felt about it. If he had felt bad, surely he would have named the city after his dead brother and called it Reme. Maybe he decided that just didn't sound as good.

Chapter 5: The Influence of Greece and Rome

Of course, there are many cities in the world, but there are not many as famous as Rome. This is because Rome once had an empire that ruled most of the world. The Roman Empire changed so much that we can still see its effects today, nearly 2,000 years later. The most obvious effect is in the languages we speak and the words we use. While languages like French and Spanish have a lot more in common with Latin, the language they spoke in Rome, English has a lot of words from Latin as well.

This is because Latin was the language of business and trade. In some ways, Latin was then what English is now. Even countries that have their own languages are influenced by English. This makes some people very annoyed, which is understandable, but it is the way things are. In the same way, many languages in the past were influenced by Latin. Some were almost totally replaced, others just took a few words. Of course, all these places knew how much influence the Greeks had on Rome as well, especially when it came to philosophy and science.

What this means is that a lot of names from the Roman and Greek myths are present in our lives today. You can see this if you look at the names of the planets: Mercury, Venus, Earth,

Mars, Jupiter, Saturn, Uranus, Neptune, Pluto (some people say that Pluto is not a planet, but whatever it is, its name comes from Rome, so I am including it here!). These names—apart from Earth and Uranus—are all the names of the Roman gods. Uranus is the name of a Greek god, but all the others are the same as the Greek gods but with different names. Venus, for example, is the Roman name for Aphrodite—the goddess of love who promised Helen to Paris. Jupiter is Zeus and Saturn is Cronus. Uranus, on the other hand, is the Greek name for the Roman god Caelus.

I will give you a warning here—some very *pedantic* people might say that the Greek and Roman gods are not always *exactly* the same. A pedantic person is someone who takes little things VERY seriously. Yes, maybe they are right about those little things, but this is a book about stories, and stories are supposed to be fun.

Maybe, when you are older, you will enjoy being pedantic. Then you can read long books about how Jupiter was only the same as Zeus in the year 341 BCE on the second Friday of June at 11:35 a.m. if you are lying down with your arm in the air. I, for example, get very angry if someone boils my egg for seven minutes instead of six minutes and thirty seconds. This is why I do not have many friends.

Mercury

Mercury is the Roman name for the Greek god Hermes. He is most famous for being the messenger god and is shown with wings on his shoes. He was fast, clever, and mischievous, which means that he enjoyed being naughty. Jupiter was his father and his mother was Maia.

Maia was not a god but a nymph. Nymphs were similar to gods but they are more associated with nature and represented things like trees or rivers. They could also represent ideas like love or, in Maia's case, growth.

Mercury was born at dawn. By lunchtime, he had invented a new musical instrument called a lyre. A lyre is a little bit like a harp. Normally they are made out of wood, but for some reason, Mercury decided to make his one out of a turtle shell. And it wasn't a turtle shell he'd found lying around, ready to be made into a lyre, either. When Mercury found it, it still had a turtle in it. I won't go into the details about what happened to the turtle, but let's just say that Mercury's first day on Earth was the poor turtle's last.

All that inventing made Mercury a little peckish and, for a young god like him the only thing that would feed his hunger was meat. Mercury wasn't happy with just going down to the local butcher, either (although, perhaps that wouldn't have been the best idea as he was still a baby and a talking, walking baby is enough to scare the bravest soldier, let alone an innocent butcher).

Instead, Mercury decided that the only thing to do was to steal some of his half-brother Apollo's best cows. So off he ran, just as the sun was going down, and herded some of the cows away from the others. He was just about to leave with the cows when he saw an old man watching him. This annoyed Mercury. He had almost gotten away with the perfect crime and now this man was a witness. He went over to the man and said, "What's your name?"

"Battus," said the old man.

"I'll give you one of these cows if you keep quiet about what you've seen," said Mercury.

Battus laughed and pointed, "See that stone over there? That stone will tell before I will."

Mercury smiled, handed over the cow to Battus, and ran away with the rest. But he stopped round the corner. He didn't trust the old man. Making sure the cows couldn't escape, he put on a hat, changed his clothes and ran in a big circle to return to Battus from the same direction he'd come from before. He put on a strange accent and said, "Hey old man. Someone's stolen my cows. You haven't seen anything have you? If you tell me, I'll give you a cow and a bull!"

Now, if you or I met two talking babies in one day, we would probably guess they were the same one, right? After all, how many talking babies can there be in the world?

Battus, on the other hand, thought one talking, cow-herding baby was nothing strange so he wasn't surprised when he met another. He did not suspect a trick. He wasn't a very honest man either so when the second baby offered him a cow and a bull, Battus pointed and said, "The other baby and all your cows went that way!"

At which point Mercury threw off his hat and his coat and said, "Ah-ha! It's me. You thought you could lie to me, did you, Battus?" And he turned Battus into a stone. Which you will either think served Battus right, or was a bit mean, depending on your point of view.

Mercury was happy turning people into stones, anyway. He ran back to the stolen cows and carried on his way, driving the cows ahead of him. He even made them walk backwards for a while to confuse anyone who followed him.

After a while he separated two unfortunate cows from the herd, drove them into a cave, wrestled them to the ground, killed, cooked, and ate them. The rest he let go, presumably terrified of the baby that had just eaten two of their friends.

Now, I don't know about you but I sometimes have difficulty getting together the energy to cook, let alone catch and butcher *and* cook my own meal. But Mercury was a god, and a very fast and strong one as well, so it isn't really fair to compare ourselves to him.

Once he had eaten enough, Mercury crept back into his mother's house and into his bed and went to sleep like nothing had happened, pretending that he was a baby like any other.

Apollo, of course, noticed that some of his cows were missing and set about tracking them down. He followed their hoofprints, looking around for someone who might have seen something but there was no one. He stopped next to a stone and sat down to rest on the way. Leaning down, he looked closer at the hoofprints and saw there were some tiny footprints in the middle of them. This made him a little suspicious. Battus thought *talking* babies were normal, but Apollo was pretty sure there weren't many *walking* babies in the world. He got up and followed the hoofprints again.

After a little bit he stopped and scratched his head. The hoofprints showed another herd of cows coming from the opposite direction! For a second he looked around, wondering which direction to go. Then he saw the tiny footprints of the baby. They were still going in the same direction. Suddenly, he realized the cows were walking backwards! Angry that someone had tried to trick him, he started following the tracks again.

Eventually he found the cave with the still hot fire and the clean bones, and found the little footprints everywhere around and guessed from the prints that this tiny baby had first fought and then eaten the cows. Now he was sure. Maybe, *maybe*, there were a couple of babies in the world who could walk, but there definitely wasn't more than one that could walk, steal cows and kill, cook, and eat them! He came to what seemed the most obvious conclusion to him—it was his new half-brother Mercury who had done this.

He went to Maia's house and went into Mercury's bedroom where he found the little god sucking his thumb and pretending to be asleep. The baby's cuteness had no effect on Apollo. He gave it a poke and said, "Hey, little brother. You better tell me what you did with my cows or I'll chuck you in prison with the Titans and even your mom and dad won't be able to get you out again."

Mercury opened his eyes and yawned and stretched and said, "Think about what you're saying, big brother. I'm a baby, how am I going to go and steal some cows and kill and eat them? That's just ridiculous. I can't even walk!"

There are a couple of problems with this answer. The main one is that if Mercury wanted to convince Apollo that he was a normal and helpless baby, he probably shouldn't have said anything at all. He should have screamed and cried and maybe drooled a bit. Those are three things that babies are good at.

Obviously, Apollo was not fooled. He laughed and said, "Oh, really? I bet you stole lots of stuff today. I bet there are shepherds and cow-herds wondering where their sheep and cows are from here to Timbuktu." Well, maybe he didn't say Timbuktu, exactly. But he would have said somewhere very far away, which is what 'Timbuktu" really means in English, even though it is a real city in Mali, Africa. What people who actually live in Timbuktu say for somewhere very far away, I do not know. New Jersey, maybe? Or Manchester? Sorry, I got distracted. Where were we? Oh, yes.

But even though he knew Mercury had done it, Apollo also knew it didn't look very good for a fully grown god to attack a baby. So he decided to go to Jupiter instead, and he told him what had happened and demanded that the baby be punished. Mercury—again, not being a very convincing baby—said, "Dad, I'm telling the truth. This guy came to my house and started accusing me of stealing his stupid cows even though you can both clearly see that I am a baby. He doesn't even have any witnesses. I swear I didn't do it."

Jupiter laughed. He didn't believe Mercury, perhaps for the obvious reason that the baby was talking long before it should have. He said, "Very clever, son. I'm very impressed. But you better tell us where those cows are."

"Okay! Fine," said Mercury, "I stole them. I'm sorry, but I was hungry. I ate two of them, but the rest just ran off. I don't know where they are."

Jupiter was impressed. Parents are often impressed by the things their children do. Sometimes they shouldn't be. But I think you will admit that what Mercury did was quite impressive. On the other hand, it is probably not a good thing for a parent to be impressed by their children's lies, but Jupiter was not a great parent. Or husband. Or son. Or friend. He wasn't a very good husband either, but that is another story.

Jupiter laughed again, "Good boy. Now go with your brother and find those cows which you stole." And he sent his two sons away.

Apollo was still very angry. His father's attitude had not helped. He made clear to Mercury that if they did not find those cows there would be trouble. He was also a little worried now. If Mercury had managed to do all this in his first day on Earth, what would he be able to do in a few years? He was just thinking about tying him up forever (the gods often look for extreme solutions) when Mercury started playing the lyre that he had made.

It was the most beautiful thing that Apollo had ever heard. He listened, amazed, until the song was finished. Then he said, "Little brother, I don't care about the cows. If you give me that lyre, we can forget about the whole thing."

Mercury looked at his older brother and smiled, "You can have it. And I'll teach you to play it beautifully as well. I'm sorry I stole your cows. I didn't mean to make you angry."

And from that day onward Apollo and Mercury were best friends. Which is probably the only time in history two gods ended an argument peacefully.

Venus

Venus is the Roman name for the Greek goddess Aphrodite. Maybe you remember her from the story of the Golden Apple. Maybe you blame her for the whole Trojan War thing. After all, if she hadn't offered Helen to Paris, a lot of problems could have been avoided. On the other hand, without her, there'd be no Rome and no Roman Empire, which might seem like a bad thing if you're Roman, but maybe not so bad if you're the rest of Europe. There are two sides to everything, after all, just like there are two sides to Janus's face.

We are going back further in time for this story about Venus, back to before the Trojan War, back to before the Golden Apple. But you might have noticed two things about Venus's personality from the story of the Golden Apple: She didn't like to hear the word no, and she wasn't afraid to cheat. Some people think cheating is very bad, but the gods don't seem to have minded it. In fact, a lot of the time they seemed to think it was funny or even clever. They thought that if you cheated and got away with it, that just meant you were smart. Which is something that a lot of people in prison thought as well. Until they ended up in prison that is. Unfortunately for the humans of mythological times, you couldn't really imprison a god, so they normally got away with it.

So you have to feel bad for the Trojan prince called Anchises. He was an honest young man. He just wanted to live a normal life, looking after his herd of cows. Most princes don't even want to look after themselves, let alone hundreds of animals, but that's the kind of man Anchises was. He used to take the cows out in the morning, make sure they had all the best grass to eat, and then bring them home again in the evening. That was what he was doing the day when Venus first saw him.

She thought he was very, *very* handsome and decided that she wanted to marry him. When she came over and said hello, Anchises thought she was very, *very* beautiful as well. So beautiful that he suspected she was a goddess.

Now, a lot of people in the myths fall in love with the gods and have no problem with it. They never seem to realize, though, that falling in love with a god rarely ends well. Take a man called Tithonus. Tithonus fell in love with the goddess Aurora and she fell in love with him. They wanted to be together forever, but Tithonus was just a man so they knew he would die one day. Aurora went to Jupiter (the Roman name for Zeus, remember) and asked him to make Tithonus immortal. The problem was that she forgot to say immortal *and forever young*! Jupiter being Jupiter, he didn't point out the mistake on her part. You can, I guess, add "bad father-in-law" to the list of things he was bad at. As a result, Tithonus lived forever but he also got older and older and older—older than anyone had ever been before. Like Ra in Egypt he ended up drooling, but he also got so weak that he couldn't move or speak. Presumably, he's still alive, and older than ever. We can agree, I think, that this was not a very nice thing for Jupiter to do. But then, we have a lot of evidence now to say that Jupiter was not a nice god.

Maybe Anchises had heard this story. Or maybe he had heard one of the many other ones where things didn't go well for a human who fell in love with a god. Or maybe he just didn't want Jupiter as a father-in-law, which seems very wise. Either way, he was pretty sure that Venus was a goddess and tried his best to stay away from her.

But we know what Venus was like, don't we? She said, "Goddess? What goddess? There aren't any goddesses around her. I'm just a princess from that town over there, here to marry you because you're the most beautiful man I've ever seen. Don't you think I'm beautiful too?"

Anchises couldn't really say anything but yes to that question. Venus was known for her beauty, after all. She could probably have won that Golden Apple without cheating if she'd been patient.

So Anchises agreed to marry Venus. He loved her, so how could he say no? Later he would say that she had lied to him, which was true, but you have to wonder, don't you, if he wasn't really lying to himself. You think you can't lie to yourself, do you? Well, you can if you want something badly enough. It's like putting your fingers in your ears and going, "LALALALALALALA," so that you can't hear the voice in your head telling you the truth. This is probably what Anchises did when it came to Venus. He knew she was a goddess but he pretended he didn't so that he could ignore the voice in his head telling him that bad things happened to people who fell in love with gods.

Venus waited until their baby, Aeneus (perhaps you remember him), was born to tell Anchises the truth.

"How could you lie to me?" he said, acting all surprised and shocked.

To which Venus probably said, "Come on! Don't pretend you didn't know. Oh, and by the way—don't EVER tell anyone Aeneus is my baby, okay. Bad things will happen if you do that." And then she left! Just like that. Gods don't often hang around once they have gotten what they want from someone.

Of course, we already know what happens when you tell someone not to do something in a myth. Yep, that's right, they do the thing they were told not to do. They might do it instantly, or maybe in a month, or maybe years later, but they will definitely do it.

In Anchises's case, it might have been understandable if the person he told about Venus was Aeneus himself. After all, a little boy is going to be curious about who their mother is. But no, Anchises just got drunk and told some people in a bar. He was just showing off. Unfortunately for him, as soon as he revealed the truth, Jupiter knew. I don't know how he overheard the conversation, but he is a god so I'm sure he has powers we don't know about. However he heard it, he was furious and threw a lightning bolt that blinded Anchises. You might feel bad for Anchises, but you have to say that Venus did warn him.

Mars

Mars is the Roman name for Ares, the god of war. The Greeks didn't actually like him that much. The Romans on the other hand thought war was the best thing there was, and that they were the best at it. That's why they said that Mars was the father of Romulus and Remus, the founders of Rome. They wanted the world to know that war was in their blood.

Mars wasn't always a great god though. One time he even got himself kidnapped by two giants and had to be saved by Mercury and Diana (the Roman name for Artemis, the goddess of the moon).

The two giants were called Otus and Ephialtes. They grew very quickly and by the time they were nine years old they were already as tall as a very tall tree. They decided they were going to fight the gods and beat them so they stacked two mountains on top of each other to reach the gods on top of Mount Olympus.

Their attack wasn't successful, but they came away with one prize: Mars, who they squeezed into a big jar and kept trapped in their house. Quite how the god of war managed to get kidnapped and stuffed into a jar by two nine-year-olds is a good question. It makes you wonder why the Romans wanted him to be their god.

However it happened, he was stuck in that jar for 13 months and would have stayed there for longer if the giants' mother, Iphimedia, hadn't heard him calling for help. She realized who it was in there and told Mercury. Why she thought she should tell on her two boys, we will never know. Maybe she just thought it was bad to keep someone in a jar.

Mercury and Diana came up with a plan to help Mars escape and went down to the giants' house. Diana went to the front door and knocked and asked to be let in. She was very beautiful and the two boys instantly fell in love with her. She chatted with them and laughed and distracted them while Mercury snuck in and grabbed the jar and ran away.

When they realized what had happened, Otis and Ephialtes were very angry with Diana. She turned into a doe, which is a female deer, and jumped between them. Both the boys tried to kill her with a spear but they missed and killed each other instead.

Mercury was waiting for her outside. He hadn't let Mars out yet because he was having too much fun laughing at him. But Diana told him to smash the jar and let their brother out. He did, and the three of them went back to Mount Olympus together.

Jupiter, Saturn, and Uranus

You already know that Jupiter is the Roman name for Zeus and Saturn is the Roman name for Cronus. Uranus, remember, is actually the *Greek* name for Caelus. We are going to talk about these three together because their story is the story of fathers and sons.

We also talked about how Jupiter fought his father Saturn, beat him, and imprisoned him. But we haven't talked about why they had a fight in the first place. It is true that this is partly because Jupiter was very ambitious and wanted to be king of the gods, but another reason is that Saturn was an even worse father than Jupiter! I know, I didn't think it was possible either. Saturn wasn't a great son either. If Jupiter might have had an excuse for fighting his father, Saturn didn't have a great one for fighting Uranus.

Uranus, the sky god, was the oldest of all the gods. He was the husband of Gaia, which was what the Greeks called the Earth. Apparently, she didn't like her husband very much, because she asked her children, the Titans, for help getting rid of him. Most of the Titans were too scared—or maybe they even loved their father, you never know—but Saturn was more than happy to help. He wanted to be king of the gods and the only way he could do that was to defeat his father.

He didn't kill him, though. He just injured him so badly that the old god was too weak to fight anymore. Uranus knew he had lost, but he had a warning for his son.

"Your own children will do the same to you as you have done to me," he said.

This worried Saturn. If he could do it, then of course his children would be able to as well.

His solution is probably the worst example of fatherhood in the history of fathers. Our parents would probably think, "Well, when I'm old, of course my children will take over from me." Or maybe they would decide they just needed to bring us up correctly, to teach us to share and to be nice, and not to fight or argue.

But we already know that Saturn didn't think like that. Just look at what he did to his own dad! Anyone who is capable of something like that is normally afraid that everyone else is just like them.

So Saturn decided he had to eat all his children as soon as they were born! He was so big that he didn't need to chew, just popped them in his mouth and swallowed, and because they were gods, they didn't die.

The childrens' mother, Rhea, wasn't too happy about this so when it came to the last one to be eaten, Jupiter, she came up with a plan. She hid the little baby away and wrapped a rock in his baby clothes instead. Saturn came as soon as he heard his wife had had another baby. He grabbed it from its bed and gobbled it up. We can assume that he didn't have a very good sense of taste because he didn't notice anything different between this one and the ones he had swallowed before. Rhea, meanwhile, took the little baby and hid him with some nymphs who kept him in a cave.

So Jupiter grew up in secret. This was easier said than done, especially when he was a baby because, as we already know, one thing babies are really good at is making a lot of noise. The nymphs came up with a plan to stop Saturn from hearing the baby screaming. They hired a load of soldiers to dance and sing every time the baby cried. They could probably have got the same result by banging some pots and pans together, but that might have driven the nymphs crazy. Not that having people singing and dancing was much better because, while babies are very good at making noise, they are also very, *very* bad at sleeping. Imagine the poor soldiers having to wake up at all hours of the day and night to drown out the noise. I wouldn't do that job if you paid me, but I'm not a very good singer or dancer, so I don't think anyone *would* pay me. On the other hand, why soldiers would be your first choice I don't know either.

Eventually, Jupiter grew up. He got hold of a drug—a drug is a type of medicine that is not always good for you—which he gave to Saturn. Presumably, Saturn was happy to drink it because he thought all the people who could hurt him, his children, were safely digesting in his stomach along with the last hotdog he ate. Unfortunately for him, this was not the case. The drug Jupiter gave him made him throw up. First came the hotdog, then the stone, then the children.

These kids were a little bit angry that he had eaten them. You would be too if your dad ate you, I'm sure. So they agreed to help Jupiter fight against Saturn and the other Titans. As we already know, that was a fight they won and the Titans were imprisoned.

Is there a lesson to be learned from this? Definitely. The lesson is be nice to your parents and your kids because if you aren't, they won't be nice to you!

Neptune

Neptune is the Roman name for Poseidon. Neptune was the god of the sea and earthquakes. He had a fearsome reputation. This means that people were very scared of him because they believed he sent sea monsters to attack their boats and even cities on the coast.

After defeating the Titans, he, Jupiter, and Pluto had put the sky, the sea, and the Underworld in a hat to see who got to be god of which. Jupiter won the sky, Pluto got the Underworld and Neptune got the sea.

He was happy with the sea, but he wanted more. He wanted to be the king of the gods and he was jealous of his younger brother. After all, who wants their little brother to be in charge of them?

For a long time he let things be, but one day Jupiter's wife Juno (the Roman name for Hera) came to him with a proposal. She was annoyed with Jupiter. He was not a good husband and was always running away with other women and goddesses. Apart from that, a lot of the gods were not happy with how Jupiter was behaving as a king. They said he was a tyrant, which means he was a cruel and unfair ruler. Juno suggested that if Neptune helped her trap Jupiter and tie him to his throne and stole the thunderbolt he got most of his power from, then Neptune could be king of the gods.

Neptune liked the sound of this. He was sick of his little brother being king. He was not the only one. He, Juno and some other gods worked to trap Jupiter and they were successful.

They weren't successful for long, though. Thetis, the mother of the Greek hero Achilles, didn't like the idea of Neptune being the king of the gods. Perhaps this was because she was herself a sea nymph and didn't like how Neptune ruled the sea. She sent a great sea monster up to Olympus to break the chains holding Jupiter down.

Jupiter had been getting angrier and angrier while he sat there chained to his throne. Now he was free he was furious and he punished the rebel gods.

He tied Juno up in the sky for a long time to think about what she had done. Neptune's punishment was more simple. He sent him to be a slave of the king of Troy for a year. This was before the Trojan War and it is because of Neptune that the war lasted so long. The king of Troy made him build the walls around the city. He built them so well that they were the strongest walls in the world. That is why the Greeks were not able to break them down and had to use the trick of the Trojan horse instead.

Pluto

Pluto, known as Hades to the Greeks, was the god of the dead. We already saw how Pluto got the Underworld, which is where people go when they die and is generally quite gloomy and dark. Hell, in other words. Pluto pretended he liked things gloomy and dark. He said he liked sad music and wore dark clothes and tried to act like being the god of the worst place in the Universe was just what he had always wanted.

But even the gloomiest person needs a bit of sunshine on their face and likes to go swimming in the warm sea. And we all like someone to sing us happy birthday and bring us a cake on our birthday. In short, even the god of the dead needs someone to love. He found it difficult, though. Most of the people he met were dead which meant they were either very old, annoyed, or very depressed about being in the Underworld. It was only natural, though definitely unfair, that they blamed Pluto for the situation they found themselves in. Added to that was the fact that looking after the Underworld was a full-time job, which meant that Pluto didn't get out much.

So when he did find the time to go into the world above he kept an eye out, searching for a beautiful woman or goddess who might like to come and live with him in the Underworld.

Up until then, the world was a very different place from the one we know now. It was summer all the time, the flowers were out, the trees had leaves on them, animals were running around in the fields. People just had no idea how depressing winter could be because they'd never seen one. There was a simple reason for this. Ceres (the Roman version of Demeter), who was the goddess of things like flowers and fruit and grain, had a daughter who made her very happy. Because she was very happy, she wanted everyone else to be happy, so she made the crops and fruit, and flowers grow all the time.

This daughter of Ceres was called Proserpina. In Ancient Greece, her name was Persephone.

Beauty might be a subjective thing, but most people agreed that Proserpina was very beautiful. Pluto certainly thought so when he saw her. In fact, he fell in love instantly. Love, you may be aware, has a habit of making people (and gods) do very stupid things. When Pluto fell in love with Proserpina he did something very stupid and, in fact, very, *very* bad. He did something you should never, *ever* do—he kidnapped her!

There are several reasons you should not kidnap someone. The first is just that it is bad. The second is that it is illegal and you will go to prison for a very long time. And the third is that if you kidnap someone, they are probably not going to like you, let alone love you. Especially if you take them straight to the Underworld. Maybe if you kidnapped them and took them to the Bahamas they would be happier, but they still will not like you.

Another reason you should not kidnap someone is that their parents are going to be very sad. They are going to wonder where their child is and be afraid that something bad, worse even than kidnapping, has happened to them. When her daughter didn't come home that evening, Ceres went out to look for her. She looked everywhere and asked everyone, but she couldn't find out where she had gone. The next day she went up to Sol, who was the god of the sun, and asked him to look for Proserpina while he crossed the sky. He could see the whole Earth from up there, so he would be able to find her easily.

Of course, the one place Sol couldn't see was the Underworld. The sun never went there, which is one of the reasons it was so gloomy. So it was that at the end of the day, when he had looked everywhere, Sol went to Ceres and said, "Sorry, I couldn't see her anywhere."

Ceres was scared for her daughter. Sometimes when people are scared, they become very angry as well. This is because they feel like they are powerless, and don't want people to know they are actually sad. They think being sad is being weak, which is not true, but people often believe things that are not true.

So Ceres was very sad and very angry. And when the gods feel something, there are consequences (normally bad ones) for the rest of us. This is because, even if they feel powerless, gods are actually very powerful. It might not have been much of a problem if Ceres was the god of something nobody likes anyway, like slugs, but she was the god of flowers and plants and crops, which basically means *food*! And when she couldn't find her daughter she said, "Until someone brings her back to me all the plants and flowers and crops will *die*!"

And they did. And all the people were very hungry because there was a famine, which is what it is called when nothing grows and there is no food.

"But it wasn't *the people's* fault," you say. I know, I agree. It seems very mean of Ceres to blame people. They didn't have anything to do with the kidnapping of her daughter. But you might have noticed by this point in the book that the gods don't really care whose fault something is. Perhaps that's why they aren't our gods anymore.

Eventually, Jupiter noticed what was going on. Personally, I think this is another black mark against Jupiter. He doesn't seem to ever pay much attention to what is happening in the world. If he wanted to be President, I wouldn't vote for him.

Unfortunately for the people in mythological times, Jupiter was the *king* of the gods, which means he didn't need people to vote for him and he could do whatever he wanted. He did at least realize that it wasn't a good thing for everybody to be hungry. They might not be able to vote for him, but they could stop worshipping him and making sacrifices to him. Why, after all, would you worship someone who lets you go hungry?

Because he was very narcissistic (remember the selfish Narcissus we spoke about at the start of the book?) and always wanted to be the center of attention, Jupiter didn't want people to stop worshipping him. Being worshipped is the best way to be the center of attention and it made him feel great.

The point is that while he didn't really care that the people were hungry, he *did* worry that they might stop worshipping him. So he looked around for Proserpina. Being the king of the gods he could see everywhere and he soon found her with Pluto in the Underworld.

Pluto was Jupiter's brother, though, so he didn't really want to annoy him by telling him to give Proserpina back. He needed Pluto to look after the Underworld. As we know, it was gloomy and depressing down there and Jupiter didn't want to have to deal with gloomy and depressing things.

Instead, he decided to delegate the job to Mercury. Delegating is when a powerful person tells someone else to do something. They do this for different reasons. Sometimes it is because they think that person has a special skill which makes them better for the job. Sometimes it is because they are busy with other, more important things. Sometimes it is because they know it is a difficult job and if it goes wrong they want to be able to point at the *other person* and say, "They did it!"

Jupiter probably delegated because he was lazy.

But whatever the reason, Mercury went down into the Underworld and spoke to Pluto. "Look, Uncle," he said. "I agree that Proserpina is very nice, but you shouldn't have kidnapped her. Ceres is furious and is causing all sorts of problems. Jupiter, well, he sent me to ask you to please, please send her back."

Now, Pluto might have been the god of the Underworld, but Jupiter was king of the gods. Pluto was just a little bit scared of his younger brother. Maybe he also thought that he owed Jupiter for saving him from Saturn's stomach!

With a sigh, Pluto agreed to give her back. He went down to Proserpina's room. He hadn't been mean to her, apart from the kidnapping. He'd actually treated her very well (not that that makes kidnapping okay!) and she didn't hate him. But she was overjoyed when he said she could go home. She got all her things together, put on her shoes, smiling and excited to see her mother and flowers and sunshine again.

"It's a long way back, though," said Pluto, "Here, have something to eat before you go." He held out his hand. In it were six red pomegranate seeds.

Now, pomegranate seeds are very tasty, but they are also very small. Why Proserpina didn't ask for a burger or some chips, I don't know. Maybe she thought it would be rude.

Either way, she smiled and said, "Thank you." And then she ate the seeds.

Perhaps you have realized by now that the gods don't do many things out of kindness. Perhaps you realized that the pomegranate seeds were a trick. You might not know why, yet, but you're smart. You know that you shouldn't accept anything from strangers, or gods, least of all a god who has kidnapped you. You were probably screaming at Proserpina to say, "Actually, I just ate, thanks. I'm stuffed! I couldn't eat anything else, even something as tiny as a pomegranate seed."

But Proserpina wasn't as smart as you. Or maybe it was just that she was very innocent and too polite for her own good. Either way, she ate the seeds and ran out of the Underworld, laughing.

Ceres was overjoyed to see her daughter again. Instantly, the flowers bloomed and the crops grew and the trees were full of fruit and nobody was hungry anymore.

But, even though she was happy, Ceres was also worried. Mothers are often worried. They are worried because they love their children and don't want bad things to happen to them. So she asked Proserpina to tell her everything that had happened in the Underworld.

When you discover that there was no reason to be worried, you are relieved. Listening to Proserpina talk, Ceres started out relieved. Pluto really had been nice to her daughter. But then, right at the end of her story, Proserpina told her about the pomegranate seeds, and Ceres was horrified!

Why was she horrified? Because she knew that if you ate anything in the Underworld you had to stay there! She could have killed Pluto!

When Jupiter heard what had happened he held up his hands and said, "Sorry, there's nothing I can do! She ate the pomegranate seeds, so she has to go back to the Underworld."

"But she only ate six!" said Ceres.

"All right," said Jupiter. "So she has to go back to the Underworld for six months every year."

Ceres didn't like this. She loved her daughter and she wanted her around all the time. But there was nothing she could do. Every year, for six months, Proserpina went to live with Pluto in the Underworld. And for those six months, no plants grew, the flowers died, and there was no fruit on the trees.

So whenever you are feeling cold and wish the sun would come out and wonder why there are no colorful flowers or oranges and apples on the trees, blame Pluto. It is his fault we have fall and winter. Those are the six months when Proserpina is with him.

It wasn't all bad, though. Proserpina, as we know, was a very nice and kind goddess. She was probably the only goddess who could ever actually like Pluto. And while we're up here suffering through the winter, Proserpina is in the Underworld, making Pluto and all the dead people very happy. She became the queen of the Underworld, and she is a good queen.

It all worked out well in the end for Pluto, then. But that does *not* make it okay to kidnap anyone.

Chapter 6: The Norse Myths

The Norsemen came from northern Europe. They are probably best known as the Vikings, who I'm sure you have heard of. They came from Denmark, Sweden, and Norway but they traveled all over the world. They invaded Great Britain, which includes England, Scotland, and Wales. This is where the English language comes from.. They invaded Ireland, Iceland and even made it as far as America nearly 500 years before Columbus did (Encyclopedia Britannica, 2018).

Just as famous as the Viking name is the fact that they were very warlike. This is a word that means they enjoyed fighting. In a lot of history classes, you will hear how they went places and killed people and destroyed their homes. Which is true. They did do all those things. The people of Great Britain, who were called the Anglo-Saxons, often complained about being attacked by the Vikings, which is funny because around 400 years earlier they had done the same to the people who lived in Great Britain before them. In fact, the Anglo-Saxons and Vikings were practically related, a bit like the Greeks and the Romans! They even had a lot of the same gods and myths.

We know their myths were very similar because they used similar names for their gods. For example, the Norse god Odin is the same as the Anglo-Saxon god Woden! Tyr, the Norse god, is the same as Tiwes, the Anglo-Saxon god. And

Thor—you've probably heard of him—is the Norse version of the Anglo-Saxon Thunor.

Have you noticed anything else about those names? What if I give you a hint?

The days of the week.

Okay, it isn't obvious at first, but if you screw your eyes up a bit and say the Anglo-Saxon names very quickly with the word 'day' after them you get our days of the week. Tuesday is 'Tiwes'-day', Wednesday is 'Woden's-day', Thursday is 'Thunor's-day', and Friday is 'Frigga's-day'!

So while you might think of Tuesday as burger day or sports day, or the day your favorite TV show is on, the Norse and Anglo-Saxon's thought of it as the day of the god Tyr or Tiwes and had lots of stories to go with it!

"Why are you telling me all this?" you're shouting, "I don't care! I'm just here for the stories."

Which is fair enough. Let's get on with the myths!

The Norse Gods

Odin

Odin was the oldest and most powerful of the gods. He was their leader, just like Zeus had been the leader of the Greek gods. There was one small difference, though: Odin took his responsibility a lot more seriously than Zeus ever did.

He worried that something bad would happen to the world—his world—one day, and he decided he had to do something to save it. He needed wisdom. He was already smart, he knew that, but he needed to be wise. With wisdom, he could protect the world from anything.

And he knew exactly where to get wisdom: at the Mimir's well. It was said that if you drank from the well you would become the wisest person in the world. Odin knew, though, that nothing was free in this world, especially not wisdom. He wondered what Mimir would want in return for a drink from the well.

Still, he decided he would do it, whatever the price. So he dressed up as an old man with a stick and went out into the world of humans and giants. When a human saw him, he looked like a human, and when a giant saw him, he looked like a giant. Nobody knew he was actually Odin, the god.

One day he met a giant and asked him who he was. The giant said, "I am Vafthrudner, who are you?"

"My name is Vegtam the Wanderer," Odin lied. Then he said, "I have heard of you, Vafthrudner. People say you are very wise."

"I'm not just very wise, I am the wisest giant that ever was."

"In that case," said Odin–*Vetgam*! I meant Vetgam, of course.

"In that case," said Vetgam, "I have a question for you."

The giant rolled his eyes. Everyone was always asking him questions. He kind of regretted his little boast about being the wisest. He said, "Okay, okay. I'll answer your question, but only if you play a game with me. We each ask each other three questions and if either of us gets one wrong, then the other one gets to chop off his head!"

Perhaps he had said it as a joke. Most people would not play a game like that with the wisest giant that ever was. It is like you or me betting an Olympic runner that we can beat them in a race—a bad idea (unless you are an Olympic runner, in which case I am very impressed. Well done).

Vafthrudner was very surprised, then, when the old giant with a walking stick agreed.

The giant looked closer at him, frowning. "Really?" He shrugged. "All right. It's your head. My first question is this: What river separates Asgard from Jötunheim?"

"Ifling," said Vegtam.

"Okay, okay," said the giant, smiling now. "Not bad. What about this: Name the horses that Dagr and Nótt ride."

Dagr was the god of the daytime and Nótt the god of the night. Each of them had a horse that they rode across the sky. Now, Vafthrudner had chosen this question because he knew that no normal man or giant could possibly answer it. Only a god or a very wise giant would know the answer. So he was very surprised when this Vegtam he had never heard of said, "Skinfaxe and Hrimfaxe."

"That's right," said Vafthrudner, probably running a finger around his collar and starting to sweat. "Yes. Wow. You're good. I'll admit that. Okay." He stopped now, thinking hard. If he couldn't catch this Vegtam out with the next question, it would put his *own* neck at risk! "Your last question then. Here it is: On which field will the last battle ever be fought?"

"Vigard," said Vegtam.

The giant laughed a little nervously, "That's right. Yes. Vigard. I'm impressed." But then he stood a little straighter. He was still the wisest giant in existence. What could this old guy ask him that he wouldn't know the answer to?

"What," said Vegtam, "are the last words Odin will whisper to his son, Baldur?"

When he heard that question the giant probably swore. He might even have shouted, or maybe he cried. He knew he couldn't answer. No one but Odin could answer that question. And as soon as he thought that he realized how stupid he had been. He pointed. "You're Odin! Only Odin could know the answer to that and only Odin would have asked that question!"

Odin smiled and said, "Maybe you're right. Maybe. But if you want to keep your head you have to tell me something: What will Mimir ask for a drink from his well of wisdom?"

The giant grumbled a little when he heard this question. He would have answered that without putting his neck in danger if he had known it was Odin asking. Gods were very annoying, he thought. They couldn't do anything the normal way. They always had to show off and make you feel small. He didn't say any of that though. After all, he now owed Odin his head, so it was best not to argue. Instead, he sighed and said, "He will ask for your right eye."

"My right eye?" said Odin. "Nothing but my right eye?"

"Yep. A lot of people and giants have gone and asked for a drink from Mimir's well. I even went myself once. But no one's ever given up their right eye. No one thinks it's worth it. I definitely didn't. Can I go now?"

Odin nodded and the giant left. He wanted to run away in case Odin changed his mind. He was too proud for that, but he did walk very, very quickly.

Odin on the other hand walked on very, very slowly. He liked his right eye. He looked at things with it. He even thought it might be better than his left eye. He tried covering one and then the other and looking at things. First, he would look at something far away, like a mountain. Then he would look at something very close, like his hand. Yes, he was sure of it. His right eye *was* better.

He sighed and walked on. He knew he should go to the well of Mimir, but he didn't want to. Instead, he just walked in circles, trying to find another solution. He couldn't. He knew there was a great fight coming, a fight between good and evil, and the only way he could save the world was to drink from that well. Then he would be so wise he would know what to do.

Finally, he forced himself to walk to the well. It had to be done. It was better to do it quickly, like pulling off a Band-Aid. The slower you do it, the more it hurts.

Mimir was standing by the well when Odin arrived. He tried not to yawn, but guarding the well was quite a boring job.

"How can *eye* help?" he said, laughing to himself. Nobody else even knew it was a joke when he said it, but he still laughed every time.

"You know what I want," said Odin. He didn't think the situation was very funny.

"All right," said Mimir, annoyed. "You know the price?"

"No," said Odin, suddenly hoping that the giant had been lying. He took out his money bag and shook it. "I've only got a few pieces of gold on me."

"It's your right eye," said Mimir, pointing at his own. "Your right eye. Nothing more, nothing less."

Odin sighed. He nodded. Then he took a deep breath and just did it.

It was not like pulling off a Band-Aid. It was a lot more painful and the pain lasted for a long time. It also took him quite a long time to get used to having only one eye. He bumped into quite a lot of things and ended up with bruises all over his right side. He did learn to live with it, though, and the pain did go away.

And it was worth it. He drank from the well and instantly he knew everything. He even saw the future. It wasn't pretty. Humanity would go through many difficult and terrible times. But he also saw how to bring an end to those times and how to save humanity.

Mimir didn't even want the eye. He threw it in the well. It's still there, floating around, staring up at anyone who looks down. It probably makes people think twice about drinking the water. Firstly, you have to give up your eye, and secondly, that water obviously isn't very clean.

Thor

The guy with the hammer! Yes, that's right. I'm sure you have heard of him. But there are plenty of stories about him I'm sure you haven't heard. He was the god of lightning and storms and, of course, thunder.

He might be most famous because of his hammer, but Thor wasn't always very careful with it. He should have been extra careful seeing as the hammer was the first line of defense for the gods' home, Asgard!

One evening he and Loki went to the giant Thrym's house for a feast. You might have heard of Loki. He was the Norse god of mischief and caused a lot of trouble. The worst trouble he was to cause was yet to come. For the moment he and Thor were best friends so they went to Thrym's feast together.

The Norse gods, just like the Vikings, liked to drink alcohol. They didn't have beer, though. They had something similar called mead. The effects of drinking mead were the same as drinking beer. Loki and Thor drank too much of it that night. So much, in fact, that they were halfway home before either of them noticed Thor's hammer was missing. Perhaps you can take this as a warning against drinking alcohol. As I'm sure you can guess, you have to be pretty stupid to forget something as big as a hammer, especially Thor's hammer. But that's what alcohol does to you, it makes you stupid. Being stupid can sometimes be fun, but generally, it is best to avoid it.

Thor was frantic with worry. He had promised never to let the hammer out of his sight and now he couldn't even remember where he had lost it. Loki, on the other hand, had obviously had a mom who had told him to retrace his steps whenever he lost something. This was good advice. Advice from moms is normally good advice.

Thor, by this point, was no use. Another thing that alcohol can do is make you very sad about very silly things and Thor was now sitting against a tree, crying. He was probably a bit scared of what Odin was going to say when he found out his son had lost the hammer.

So Loki ran to the palace where all the gods lived and up the stairs to speak to Freyja. She had a special coat made of falcon feathers. Anyone who wore the coat could fly. Loki asked to borrow it from her so he could fly back to the giant Thrym's house and look for the hammer.

Freyja knew how important the hammer was. She probably also knew how furious Odin would be if he ever found out it was gone, so she didn't hesitate to hand it over.

Loki flew back to Thrym's house but he found him outside in the garden, putting the leashes on his dogs so they could go for a walk. I don't know if you are a cat person or a dog person. Maybe you are a lizard or a snake person. Or maybe you prefer spiders. Whatever kind of animal you like, you know that sometimes people speak to their pets. It is silly. Obviously, they can't understand us. But we do it anyway. Thrym was no different. Loki, dressed as a falcon and sitting in a tree, heard him talking to his dogs.

"I'll be able to get you some nicer collars soon, boys," he told them. "Don't you worry. Now that I've got Thor's hammer, things are going to get a lot better for us!"

"Ha!" said Loki, jumping out of the tree. "You might have the hammer, Thrym, but we know you have the hammer and we'll find out where you've hidden it no problem!"

Thrym was a little surprised, it's true, but then he laughed. "Search all you like, Loki. You'll never find it. I've buried it eight miles under the earth."

Loki pursed his lips and put his hands on his hips. "So there's no point looking for it then, is there?"

"Nope," said Thrym, grinning.

"What do you want for it, then? Gold? How about this falcon feather coat? Have you ever flown? It's amazing."

"I don't want any of those," said Thrym. "I'll never give the hammer back."

"Come on, Thrym, my old friend." Loki put an arm around the giant's shoulders. "There must be something."

"Well," said Thrym, blushing and twisting the dogs' leash between his fingers. "Freyja is very beautiful, you know."

Loki smiled and winked. "She is, isn't she?"

"I guess, if you get her to be my wife, I might think about giving the hammer back."

As soon as he heard this Loki said, "Don't worry—you'll soon be married!"

And jumping into the air, he flew away, straight to the palace.

By the time he got back, everyone had heard what had happened. It is easy to notice an enormous hammer, especially when Thor is supposed to have it with him *at all times.*

"What did he say, Loki?" they asked him, as soon as he had taken his coat off.

Loki cleared his throat. Freyja was there with the rest of them, waiting to hear what Thrym had said. Loki avoided her eyes. "Well, he said... He said he would give it back if Freyja married him. So I promised him she would." He was speaking very quickly when he finished and made sure to be far away from Freyja.

He was right to be nervous. Freyja was disgusted and angry. "What! How dare you offer me as a wife like some kind of..." She was so angry she didn't know what to say for a moment, but then she spoke again, "Never! I will never marry that stupid little giant!"

Then Heimdall, the gatekeeper of the gods had an idea. "Why don't we just dress someone else up as the bride. If we put Freyja's necklace on them, Thrym will think it's her and won't notice until it's too late, after we've got the hammer back."

"Hey," said Loki, nodding. "That's actually a good idea. Who?"

Now, what I am about to tell you might seem a bit strange. I mean, Thrym wasn't blind, and there were plenty of other goddesses who could have pretended to be Freyja. If the plan was just to get the hammer back and then run away, why couldn't Freyja just pretend to get married and then run away with the hammer?

But as you might have noticed, the gods do not go for the obvious solution. They go for the craziest one they can think of, which in this case meant dressing Thor up as Freyja. Loki, who was a pretty skinny guy, would have made a lot more sense. But even with a veil, it is hard to imagine anyone could have confused Thor for Freyja.

Maybe the gods just wanted to punish Thor for losing the hammer. He certainly wasn't happy to be dressed up like that. Loki, who promised to go with him as his maid-servant, was a lot more comfortable about it and was actually quite enjoying himself.

So the two of them went off to the wedding, the other gods laughing about how beautiful the bride looked, Thor trying not to trip in his high-heels.

A tear appeared in Thrym's eye when he saw his bride. The ceremony was beautiful and all the giants were full of joy at the happy occasion. After the ceremony, there was the feast.

Thor had learned nothing from the whole experience up to this point. He ate and he drank, he ate and he drank. He ate (apparently) one whole cow, eight salmon, and all the little snacks. To wash that down, he drank three tonnes of mead!

"Have you ever seen a woman eat and drink so much!" said Thrym, very impressed. He was so impressed that he tried to sneak a kiss but jumped back when he saw his new bride's eyes. "Wow! I've... I've never met a woman with such," he cleared his throat, trying to think of a polite word, but he couldn't, "*scary* eyes!"

Loki, still dressed as a maid-servant, jumped in and said, "Oh, that's just because she's very, very tired, you see. She hasn't slept for eight nights because she's been so excited about marrying you!"

Thrym frowned, trying to catch glimpses under the veil, but Thor just giggled and pretended to be shy. Thrym smiled. "Okay. That's understandable. Oh, by the way—and what about the *dowry*?"

A dowry was a gift that the bride's family gave to the groom when they got married. As Freyja was one of the gods, Thrym was expecting a lot of gold. If we are honest, he was just as excited about this as he was about marrying the goddess of his dreams.

Loki held up a finger. "No dowry until we get that wedding gift you spoke about with Loki."

"The hammer?" said Thrym. "A deal's a deal, I guess." He waved one of his servants over and said, "Go and get the hammer."

While they waited they drank and ate some more. Once again, we can probably blame the alcohol for Thrym not noticing that his new wife had very muscly arms, a very deep voice, and a beard.

Loki was sweating under his dress. It was a very hot dress, it is true, but mostly he was sweating because he was scared the giant would realize he had been tricked before the hammer arrived. Thor, on the other hand, was not the type of god to worry. He just kept drinking and eating.

"Here it is." The servant returned, holding out the hammer.

Loki almost laughed with relief.

Thor jumped up, grabbed the hammer, threw back his veil and, with a great big smile on his face, began smashing up everything in Thrym's house, starting with Thrym himself.

Loki rolled his eyes and went outside to wait.

Tyr

Tyr was the bravest of the Norse gods. You might be thinking, "What an idiot! No, he wasn't, that was Thor. I've seen the movies."

You're right, Thor was very brave. But he wasn't as brave as Tyr. When they heard about Tyr, the Romans thought he must be the same as their god Mars. And Mars was their favorite god, so this meant they were very impressed.

That's not the main reason we know he was the bravest, though. We know he was the bravest god because of how he tricked the great wolf, Fenrir, who was Loki's son.

Loki had three children with the witch, Angerboda.

One of their children was a giant snake called Jörmungand. Thor had no difficulty dealing with the snake. He grabbed it by the tail, swung it around his head a few times, and threw it into the sea. It wasn't a perfect solution! The snake liked it at the bottom of the sea and grew until it reached around the Earth. It was, however, at the bottom of the sea, so the gods felt like they didn't have to worry about it anymore.

Loki and Angerboda's second child was a girl called Hela. The gods were terrified of her because half of her was a normal woman and the other half was dead! If she looked at you from the right side, she had healthy skin and a beautiful blue eye. If she looked at you from the left, there was just bone and teeth and a black, empty eye socket.

We should not judge anyone by how they look. It is very rude and is also not a very reliable way to decide if someone is good or bad. I myself have broken a few mirrors in my time, but I promise I am a very nice person and quite a good cook. If you decided you didn't like me because of how I looked we would never be friends and you would never get to eat my famous spaghetti.

The Norse gods were powerful and intelligent and beautiful, but I don't think they were very nice. They didn't want Hela anywhere near them, so Odin took Hela and threw her into the caves under the Earth.

Hela didn't seem to mind this too much. She made her own world down there and made herself queen of it. This is where our word *hell* comes from. The Norse gods said that it was a nasty place down in her world, but the Norse gods only liked people who enjoyed fighting and killing, so maybe Hela's world was actually quite nice! As we mentioned before, beauty is a question of opinion.

"You were supposed to be telling us about Tyr and Fenrir!" you say? I am getting there. I just wanted to tell you about his brother and sister first because the other gods weren't afraid of them—at least, not so afraid that they wouldn't even touch them.

They *were* too afraid to touch the wolf Fenrir. Fenrir was very powerful and loved destroying things. That sounds bad, I know, but I think you'll agree that sometimes breaking stuff can be fun.

The only one who wasn't scared of Fenrir was Tyr. He still couldn't control him, exactly, but he could calm him down so that he wouldn't break too much stuff. He did this by feeding him some nice, raw meat every day. He stuck it on the end of his sword and held it out for Fenrir to eat.

Perhaps you have a dog, or a cat, or a spider. If you feed them, they start to like and trust you. It was the same with Fenrir and Tyr.

That didn't stop the wolf from destroying things, though. Eventually, the gods decided something had to be done. They decided to tie the wolf up so he couldn't break any more stuff.

They had a slight problem, though. They were all too scared to go near Fenrir.

They had a plan, though. They knew Fenrir was proud of his strength, so they challenged him. They made the thickest, strongest chain they could and then they went to Fenrir and said, "Wow. Fenrir. Wow, you really are *strong*. But how strong are you exactly? I bet you couldn't break these chains if we tied you up."

Fenrir laughed and said, "Of course I can!"

And he lay down and let them tie him up. Standing, dusting their hands, the gods smiled. But then Fenrir broke the chains and they stopped smiling. Fenrir really was strong. They were right to be scared of him.

So they tried again. They made a new chain, thicker and stronger, and they tried again. "Hey, Fenrir," they said. "Okay, you broke that last one, it's true. But what about this chain?"

Fenrir snorted. These gods were idiots, he thought. "Look, I'm *Fenrir*, okay? There is no chain that I can't break."

"You're just scared. I told you he couldn't break it," the gods said to each other.

"Of course I can break it!" snapped Fenrir. And he lay on the ground again and let them chain him up.

The gods stood up, dusting their hands. They weren't smiling this time, they were just hoping—hoping Fenrir couldn't break the chain.

But he could and he did, easily.

prove I can break that? I've just broken two massive chains! Obviously, I can break that piece of string."

The gods said, "Well... No... I mean. Yes, it's a piece of string, but it's really strong. Like a spider's cobweb. It looks thin and weak, but if you get a load of it together it's pretty strong, you know?"

Fenrir narrowed his eyes. He sensed a trick. "I bet there's something magic about that string. No, I'm not letting you put that on me. I'm not stupid. I'm strong, yes, but I can't break a magical piece of string."

"There's nothing magical about this piece of string. We promise, Fenrir."

Fenrir said, "Well, I don't trust you. I'm not going to do it."

Tyr came forward. He said, "You trust me, don't you Fenrir?" Fenrir still wasn't sure, but Tyr kept talking, "How about this: I will put my hand in your mouth while they tie you up, and then if there's anything magical about the string, you can bite my hand off!"

Fenrir agreed. Tyr came forward and put his hand between the wolf's fangs. "Not your left hand," Fenrir mumbled, slobbering all over the hand. "Your right hand." He knew Tyr was right-handed and that the right hand was worth a lot more to him.

Tyr switched his hands and stood still and calm while the other gods tied the string around Fenrir.

When it was all around him, Fenrir tried to break the string. He tried and he tried but he couldn't do it. That was how he knew he had been tricked. He would have been able

The gods threw up their hands. This plan clearly wasn't working. They needed something stronger than a chain. And they knew who to go to—the dwarves.

The dwarves listened to the gods' order, nodding as they did. "Yes," they said. "We can make something that will keep Fenrir tied up, no problem. We will make it out of six things."

"Which six things?" said the gods, worried about the price.

"The roots of stones, the breath of a fish, the beards of women, the noise made by the footfalls of cats, the sinews of bears, the spittle of a bird," (Colum, 1920).

"The roots of stones? Beards of women? But fish can't breathe," said one god.

"And I've never heard the footfalls of a cat!" said another.

"Sounds expensive," said a third.

"Do you want Fenrir tied up or not?" said the dwarves.

"Fine," said the gods. "Whatever the price. It'll be worth it."

So the dwarves set about collecting the six things. Where they got them, we don't know. Sometimes it's important to keep things secret. If the dwarves revealed where they got the materials, then the gods could have made the chain themselves!

What they made wasn't exactly a chain, though. In fact, it was more like a piece of string. At first, the gods thought they had been tricked. Then, the dwarves said, "Just try it out. You will see that it is the strongest material in the world."

There was another problem. When the gods took the string to Fenrir he looked at it and said, "Why do you need me to to break any normal string. So, furious, he bit Tyr's hand clean off.

Now, when you see a picture of Tyr, you will see that he only has one hand. He sacrificed his other hand so that Fenrir couldn't destroy the world anymore.

Chapter 7: The Celts

When most people hear the word *Celtic* they think *Irish*. If you said that to a Scottish or Welsh person, they would probably be quite annoyed, as they are also Celtic cultures. If you had said, "Celtic just means Irish," a thousand years ago, *a lot* of people would have been annoyed because back then the Celts were spread all across Europe (Proinsias, n.d.).

They gradually got squeezed into the corners of Europe, first by the Romans, then by the Germanic people like the Anglo-Saxons, and of course the Vikings. Now they are only found in a couple of very western parts of the continent. You can often tell where the people have a Celtic background because they have two languages: The main language of the country and a Celtic language.

These places are very proud of their Celtic roots. This is often because these countries were invaded by other places over the centuries but always kept their own sense of identity. And perhaps this is one reason why people think of Ireland when they think of the Celts; just as Alexander the Great and the Romans used their myths to connect themselves to gods and heroes, so the Irish used theirs.

The Irish did this a lot more recently though. In the 20th Century they did this with the main aim of separating themselves from the British Empire. During this period, writers, teachers and politicians used the old language, sports, culture and myths of Ireland to recreate the Irish identity and to make sure it was very different from that of the British Empire. As a result, the Irish myths have been told many more times, by many more people and are the most famous. These are the myths we are going to look at in the next part of this book.

Their myths are full of giants and warrior queens and gods and goddesses and sacred bulls and magical salmon and all sorts of crazy things. But for any country that wants to free itself from the control of another, the things it needs most of all are heroes. Luckily for the Irish, their myths had plenty of those.

Celtic Heroes

Cú Chulainn

One of the most famous Irish heroes is Cú Chulainn (which is more or less pronounced "coo-hull-un"). His exploits, or adventures, started when he was very young and carried on right until he died which, coincidentally, was also when he was very young.

No one is quite sure who exactly Cú Chulainn was, which is to say that no one was sure *what* he was. Some people say he was the son of Dechtire and the Celtic god Lugh of the Long Arm. Other people say he was actually Lugh in human form.

Whether he was a god or a demi-god, all the myths agree that Cú Chulainn was very strong, very handsome, and very smart. He was blessed with seven fingers on each hand and seven toes on each foot. He even had seven pupils! This was supposed to make him better than normal people like you and me, although you could probably argue that having seven of any of those things would be more of a problem than a help. Having seven fingers would just get in the way. And where are you going to find shoes that fit seven toes?

For Cú Chulainn, though, having all these extras was a big help in performing some of greatest deeds. He is most famous for defeating the army of Queen Maebh single-handedly when he was just seventeen. You might think that one person, even one god, couldn't defeat a whole army. But, apart from being strong, handsome, smart and having all those extra fingers, toes and pupils, he was also a berserker.

Berserker is a viking word for a warrior who goes so crazy when they fight that it is impossible to stop them. The stories say that Cú Chulainn's eyes would bulge and his muscles would expand and his veins would stick out like ropes when this happened to him. You didn't want to be anywhere near Cú Chulainn when he went berserk because he would pretty much kill anything in sight, and those seven pupils meant that he could see a lot of things!

But Cú Chulainn was famous long before he fought Queen Maebh's army and there are many stories about his boyhood and even how he was born.

The Birth of Cú Chulainn

The confusion about whether he was a god or a demi-god probably comes from the circumstances around his birth, which were far from normal. His uncle, Conchubar, was king of Ulster in the north of Ireland and was having a feast to celebrate his sister Dechtire's marriage to a man named Sualtim. As you might have noticed, this is not the name of Cú

Chulainn's father, and that is because the wedding did not go ahead as planned. In fact, it went very, very wrong.

Dechtire was celebrating with everyone else, dancing and chatting and having fun. All the excitement left her very thirsty and so she went to get a drink. Being all excited, and perhaps already a little drunk (the Celts enjoyed a drink just as much as the Norsemen), she didn't notice the mayfly that had landed in it. She swallowed the fly.

If this were anything other than a myth, she would have made a face, drunk some more and carried on having fun. But you know that isn't what is going to happen here. Instead, she became very tired and had to go and lie down. Being a queen, she couldn't go and lie down all by herself, so 50 of her friends went with her.

While she was sleeping, Lugh appeared in her dreams. He said, "That wasn't just any old mayfly you swallowed, Dechtire. That was me. And now you, and all your friends, have to come with me."

And he turned them all into the most beautiful birds. We don't know which kind, exactly, but myths tend to have people turn into swans, so if you want to picture it, picture 51 swans taking off across the sky.

Conchubar and Sualtim had no idea what had happened. They went and looked in Dechtire's room and she wasn't there. Nor were any of her friends. It was the greatest mystery of the age and it took a whole year before it was solved.

Aside from missing 50 of their number, life for Conchubar and his kingdom returned to normal until one day a flock of beautiful birds appeared from the sky and started to destroy and eat all the crops and plants.

As beautiful as the birds were, the sight of all their hard work and food being destroyed angered Conchubar and his men. They ran outside shooing the birds away. After the birds had flown off, the men decided getting rid of them wasn't enough. They jumped in their chariots and chased after the flock, admiring them all the time but still determined to make sure they never came back.

By nightfall, they still hadn't caught up with the birds, so they decided to find somewhere to sleep. Luckily, there was a castle nearby that they went to see if they could sleep there.

A man answered the door. He was young, strong, handsome and wearing armor. There was a woman standing next to him. Conchubar and his friends asked if they could stay the night. The young man laughed. "Don't you recognize this woman?"

The men looked at her for a moment. They shrugged. They didn't recognize her.

"Aren't you missing 51 women?" said the young man.

"Yes, we are," said one of Conchubar's men.

"So look again!"

Suddenly one of Conchubar's men, who had been standing at the back shouted, "That's my girlfriend!"

The young man laughed again. "It is!"

"So you have my sister too?" said Conchubar.

"She is here, but she can't see you now."

"Why not?"

"She is giving birth. But come in, have some food, have a rest."

If you or I suddenly discovered 51 of our loved ones after a year, we would probably call the police. Conchubar and his friends didn't seem to find the whole situation too strange, though, because they went in, ate, drank and slept, no questions asked.

Conchubar was the first to wake up in the morning. He went looking for the young man whose castle it was, but couldn't find him anywhere. No one ever saw him again. Instead, Conchubar heard a baby crying and followed the cries to find Dechtire with a baby.

And that is how Cú Chulainn came into the world. This explains why some people think he is just a demi-god and other people suspect he might be an actual god. After all, what happened to the young man of the castle?

Either way, Cú Chulainn went home with his mother and grew up with her and his step-father Sualtim. He wasn't called Cú Chulainn yet, though. When he was young he was known as Setanta. How he got his name is another story, which we will get to now.

How Cú Chulainn Got His Name

The Romans never made it to Ireland, but they came across the Celts in Britain and heard about the god Lugh from there. They decided that he must be the same as their god Mercury. This makes sense when you hear about Cú Chulainn's personality. Whether you think he is Lugh or is just his son, he is bound to have many of his characteristics. It is both a curse and a blessing that we all have things in common with our family.

And, if you remember what Mercury was like, you will remember that he was precocious. Precocious means that you are doing things people do not normally do until they are older (such as running around, stealing cows and turning old men into stone). Cú Chulainn was precocious too. He was very strong and smart and could defeat boys much older than him at sport and fighting when he was still very young. He would often travel around on his own, visiting people and having adventures.

When he was around seven, he went to stay with uncle, Conchubar. He hoped to be a great warrior one day and he thought it was more likely to happen living there. There were also other boys there who he could play games with. They were much older than him, but still he beat them easily, often playing with him on one team and everyone else on the other. He was one of those annoying people who was good at everything they did.

His favorite sport was hurling. Hurling is an Irish sport where each player has a stick called a hurley and two teams of hurlers try to score goals with a ball like a baseball. One day, while he was playing (and winning) his uncle called out that he was going to see a friend of his called Culain. Cú Chulainn was enjoying his game too much to leave just then and shouted back that he would come later, following his uncle's chariot tracks to find the way.

"All right," said his uncle. "But don't come too late. Culain has a guard dog, a hound the size of a shed with teeth as long as your arm. It has killed many intruders and the whole country is afraid of it. Culain puts him out as soon as the sun goes down."

Cú Chulainn shouted "Okay!" It wasn't long at all before his mind was already back in the game. Conchubar left him there and went to see his friend.

Even if he was precocious, Cú Chulainn was still a young boy, and young boys do not often pay attention to what adults tell them. He had not paid attention to his uncle's warning and continued playing until late in the day.

Eventually he set off, playing a game he liked to play to make a journey more fun. He would hit the hurling ball as far and high as he could then throw his stick after it and run after them, catching both before they hit the ground. That made the time pass faster for him. The sun began to go down as he went, and it was starting to get dark by the time he arrived at Culain's castle. Everyone was inside. The guard dog was prowling around the garden, ready to attack anyone it saw.

Unfortunately for the dog, the next person it saw was the little boy, Cú Chulainn. It ran at him, spit flying from its fangs, ready to eat him. Cú Chulainn wasn't afraid. He was almost never afraid. He took his hurley and hit a ball at the dog. He hit it so hard that the dog died! Which seems a little unfair, since it was only doing its job. Yes, people were terrified of it, but that's exactly what you want from your guard dog.

Inside the castle they heard a howl. Conchubar turned to Culain in horror, "I forgot my nephew was coming after me! He's been killed!"

When Cú Chulainn marched through the door without a scratch on him, the horror turned to anger. You might think that Cú Chulainn's uncle would be happy that his nephew hadn't been eaten, but actually he was more annoyed that his friend's dog was dead. He knew Culain would never find another one like it. He told the little boy off.

Cú Chulainn felt bad and promised to train a puppy to be a new guard dog for him. He also promised that, until the puppy was grown and ready, he would guard Culain's house and cows and property himself.

Culain accepted the offer and said, "From now on, you will be called Cú Chulainn—the *Hound of Culain*."

"I don't know, I'd rather keep my old name—Setanta," Cú Chulainn said.

Culain shook his head. "Don't be silly. One day the whole world is going to know the name Cú Chulainn!"

Cú Chulainn thought about it before saying, "Well, if it'll make me famous, I'll keep it."

Which is why we are talking about Cú Chulainn instead of Setanta right now!

Fionn MacCumhaill

Fionn MacCumhaill (or Finn McCool) was another very famous Celtic mythological hero of Ireland. He was the leader of a group of soldiers called the Fianna, who had many great exploits. In some stories, he is described as a giant (as was Cú Chulainn at times). He was said to be descended from druids and was very wise.

How he became so wise is a story in and of itself. When he was a boy, Fionn went to learn poetry from the poet Finnéces. The poet lived by the River Boyne. He had been living there for seven years, trying to catch the great salmon of wisdom that lived in a deep part of the river called Fec's Pool. Once he caught the salmon, he would eat it and then he would know everything there was to know in the world.

So Fionn lived with Finnéces and did all the dirty work for him, things like making fires and cooking and cleaning the tent. Anything the poet told him to do, he did it. Then, one day, after many years and even more hours of boredom fishing for the salmon (Odin just had to give up his eye, which was painful, yes, but also quick), Finnéces finally caught it.

He gave the salmon to Fionn to cook, with a warning not to eat it. It was a big salmon, plenty for both of them, but whoever ate the first bite would take all the knowledge. Of course, Finnéces didn't tell Fionn that.

Now, you might be thinking that you know what happens when people are told not to do something in a myth. 99 times out of 100 they do it. But Fionn was an obedient boy, which means that he did what he was told. Unfortunately for Finnéces, but fortunately for Fionn, he burned his thumb on the salmon while he was cooking it. The burn hurt so much that Fionn instantly stuck his thumb in his mouth to cool it down. The problem was that the thing that had burned him was a drop of grease and in that drop of grease was all the wisdom in the world. Fionn, sucking his thumb, suddenly knew everything there was to know about the past, present, and future. From that moment on, whenever he had a question, he just had to suck his thumb to find out the answer.

You have to feel sorry for Finnéces, though. Fionn brought him the salmon and the poet grabbed it and took a big bite, expecting to become the wisest man in history. But nothing happened. Then he looked up and saw the strange new look in Fionn's eyes and realized that all the wisdom was in the boy. Poor Finnéces. He threw the plate of salmon away and walked off in a huff.

Fionn left the poet and went on to have many great adventures. He built the Giant's Causeway, which you can still visit if you are ever in Northern Ireland, and became a great king. There was only one person he was afraid of, someone we have already met: Cú Chulainn.

Now, it often happens in mythology that a character changes. In later stories, they might be a giant, like Fionn or Cú Chulainn, when they had been a warrior or demi-god in others. This is because people always like to exaggerate. This is a bit like lying, but not quite. Maybe you have a friend at school whose stories you do not believe. They are always telling you about some amazing thing their mom or dad did but it seems impossible. It might be a lie, in which case none of it is true, or it might be an exaggeration, in which case some of it might be true. For example, their mom or dad probably did really catch a very big fish, it just wasn't nearly as big as a car.

Another thing that happens in myths is that a character who is a hero in one story will become the villain or bad guy in another. How does this happen? Maybe it is like the broken telephone game. Have you ever played that game? You whisper something like, "I like chocolate," to one person, and they whisper what they heard to the person next to them and *they* whisper what *they* heard to the person next to them until it gets to the last person who thinks you said, "My bike has a lock on it."

Well, a similar thing can happen with stories over the years, and if there is enough time and enough people tell them, they can change completely. Perhaps that is how in the story we are about to read, Cú Chulainn got a magic finger to match Fionn MacCumhaill's, only Cú Chulainn's gave him strength rather than wisdom. And perhaps that is also how Cú

Chulainn, who was a hero before, became a villain to Fionn MacCumhaill.

However it happened, Fionn was terrified of him. One day Fionn was sucking his thumb and it told him that Cú Chulainn was coming to kill him. Fionn ran home to his wife Oonagh and said, "What am I going to do? What am I going to do? He's coming to kill me!"

Oonagh, who was smarter than Fionn, despite all the wisdom he had in his thumb, said, "Don't worry, love, I've got a plan."

She told Fionn to go and get into the baby's bed, leftover from when their son had been little. She dressed her husband in baby clothes and pulled the blankets up to his chin.

Now, we've come across this a couple of times in the myths in this book. Something that seems so crazy there is no way it could work. We weren't fooled by Thor dressing up as Freyja, but Thrym was, and we weren't fooled by Mercury the talking baby either. You might be thinking now, how could Fionn, a GIANT, pretend to be a baby?

I don't know. It is very strange. But it worked, as we will see. You will just have to suspend your disbelief, which is a very complicated way of saying to forget that this is silly.

Cú Chulainn arrived and knocked on the door. "Is this Fionn MacCumhaill's house?" he shouted.

Oonagh came out and said, "Oh, hello. Yes it is, but he isn't in at the moment. You could wait here with me and the baby until he gets back."

"That would be nice, thanks," said Cú Chulainn. He went over to take a look at the baby. "He's a big one, isn't he?"

"Yes, he is. Big and strong." Oonagh smiled, and asked, "Care for a cup of tea?"

"Yes, please."

"Ah," she said, sounding annoyed. "It's so dark in here. I've been asking Fionn to turn the house around so the sun comes in through that window for ages now, but he never does it. I'll do it tomorrow, he says. What good is tomorrow?"

"I could do it for you if you like," offered Cú Chulainn.

"Would you?" said Oonagh.

Cú Chulainn cracked the knuckle of his right middle finger three times. Then he went outside, picked up the house with Fionn and Oonagh still in it, and turned it around so that the sunlight came in through the window.

Fionn was even more scared now. "Get rid of him, Oonagh," he whispered.

"Didn't you see, Fionn? He cracked his finger three times, that is where he gets his strength and power from, just like you get your wisdom from your thumb!"

Then Cú Chulainn came back in and sat down so they had to be quiet.

Oonagh said, "I'm just going to make some muffins, if you'd like one."

"Sounds delicious," said Cú Chulainn.

Now, Oonagh wasn't just going to make any old muffins. She made two batches, carefully keeping what she was doing hidden from her guest. In one batch of muffins, she put some rocks in the middle so that they were very hard. The others she made like normal. They were chocolate muffins. Those were Fionn's favorite.

When they were ready, she gave Cú Chulainn one of the ones with rocks in and a normal one to Fionn.

Cú Chulainn shouted in pain when he bit into his muffin. "I've lost a tooth! What do you put in these?"

"What are you talking about? They're just normal muffins. Look, the baby's eating them fine." She pointed to Fionn who was munching happily on his muffin, chocolate rubbed all over his face so that he looked more like a baby.

Cú Chulainn was very impressed. "He must have very strong teeth," he said. He went over to the baby's bed and stuck a finger—the finger from which all his strength came—into Fionn's mouth to check his teeth.

Fionn bit his finger off. Cú Chulainn instantly lost all his power and Fionn jumped out of the bed and said, "It's me! And now you are powerless and I can defeat you, Cú Chulainn!"

Which he did. He killed him, actually. Which seems a bit mean. Cú Chulainn was powerless now, so Fionn didn't have to kill him.

Maybe Cú Chulainn wasn't the villain in this story, then? Maybe it was Fionn. Do you see how confusing these things can be?

Oisín

Ireland is famous for its writers and poets and it always has been. A lot of the Irish poets are seen as heroes too. One of the most famous heroes of all was the poet Oisín. Oisín was the son of Fionn MacCumhaill, but in the myths he had just as many, if not more, adventures and was respected as much as his father.

Oisín is best known for his journey to Tír ná nÓg and his love for Niamh. This is the story we will tell here.

Tír ná nÓg means the Land of Youth in English. When you were there you aged so slowly that it was like living forever. The king of Tír ná nÓg, Niamh's father, was a paranoid man. He constantly worried about things when there was not really anything to worry about. One of his biggest worries was that someone would steal his crown.

The phrase "steal his crown" does not mean take the gold crown off his head and run away with it. It actually means to take his place as king. He asked his druid if he should be worried about this.

The druid said, "You don't have to worry about anyone stealing your crown. Oh, unless your son-in-law takes it from you. Sorry, I almost forgot to mention that part."

The king laughed. He didn't have a son-in-law so he felt a lot better about the whole thing. But then he saw his daughter, Niamh, and he started to worry. She was smart, she was beautiful, and she was a princess. Her beauty worried him most of all. He didn't have a very high opinion of young men. He thought that beauty was the main thing they wanted in a wife. This was probably because that was the main thing *he* had wanted from his wife.

So he had some words with his druid. The druid suggested that they turn Niamh into a pig. Then she wouldn't even be human and no man would ever marry her. The king thought about this but then decided it was too cruel.

"No," he said. "That's too much. Just give her a pig's head."

The druid nodded and said, "Your wish is my command—"

No. Wait. Sorry, that's from Aladdin.

The druid nodded and said, "A pig's head. Not a problem."

And the next day, Niamh woke up with a snort. Which is something a lot of us do after a long night snoring, but the difference here was that Niamh couldn't stop. She looked in the mirror and found that the druid had done what her father had asked. She still had her old body, it was true, but in the place of her head was that of a pig.

When the druid saw how sad the poor girl was, he felt very sorry for her. One day, when the king was busy somewhere else, he called Niamh to him and whispered, "Look, you don't have to be this way forever, you know?"

Niamh snorted with excitement, then covered her nose and said, "Really?"

"Really. All you have to do is marry one of Fionn MacCumhaill's sons. Do that and the pig's head will be gone and you'll be back to normal."

"One of Fionn MacCumhaill's sons? Where can I find one of them?" Niamh asked.

"They're from Ireland."

The words were barely out of his mouth before Niamh was gone. How exactly she got to Ireland, we don't know. If everyone knew the way to Tír ná nÓg, the place would be crowded with people who want to live forever.

When she arrived in Ireland, Niamh walked all over the island asking people if they knew Fionn MacCumhaill or any of his sons. Some people said that no, sorry, they didn't. Others said they had seen Fionn going in the opposite direction, or that they hadn't seen him for a while. A lot of people screamed and ran away when Niamh put her hood down and revealed her pig's head. This isn't necessarily because they thought she was ugly; they just thought it was terrifying that anybody had a pig's head instead of their own. They probably would have been just as scared of a pig with a person's head.

Oisín, meanwhile, was out hunting. He was such a good hunter that he ended up with a small mountain of dead pheasants, boar, and deer. There were so many that his servants threw up their hands and said it was too much to carry. They left him there with his dogs, wondering what to do. It would be a terrible thing to leave so much food when so many people were going hungry.

Niamh saw him standing there, thinking. She went up to him and asked, "Excuse me. You don't happen to know Fionn MacCumhaill, do you?"

Oisín looked up to see who had spoken. He couldn't help but jump with fright when he saw the pig's head, but he was polite, so he tried to pretend he had meant to jump by doing some jumping jacks.

When he had finished, he said, "Sorry, I was just doing some warm-ups before I try to carry all this stuff home." He pointed to the dead animals.

"There's certainly a lot to carry," said Niamh. "So, do you know Fionn MacCumhaill?"

"I do, actually. He's my dad."

"Really?" said Niamh. She took a closer look at Oisín. He was handsome and strong, she thought. Not that any of that mattered. She would have married almost anyone to get rid of the pig's head. "Tell you what, I'll help you carry all this if you take me to Fionn."

"That would be great!" Osin happily agreed. "I was worried it would all go to waste."

So they bundled up the game and set off walking through the forest.

As they walked, they chatted and got to know each other. Oisín laughed a lot and found himself thinking that Niamh was quite cute when she laughed too, even though she snorted. She knew some great poems as well, which Oisín liked as he was a poet. He found himself enjoying her company so much that he took her the long way home.

It was starting to get dark when he said, "You aren't any normal woman, are you Niamh?"

"Was it the pig's head that gave it away?" said Niamh, laughing.

"No. I mean, yes—that is unusual. But you're different in other ways too. I like you."

"I like you too, Oisín," said Niamh, and it was true. "You're right, I am different. My father's the king of Tír ná nÓg. He put this stupid head on me and the only way I can get rid of it is if one of the sons of Fionn MacCumhaill agrees to marry me."

Oisín was smart enough to recognize a marriage proposal when he heard one, even if it was a little strange. He turned to her, grinning. "Right here and now. Let's get married!"

The game was forgotten. They ran to find a druid and were married before nightfall. Niamh got her normal head back and they were both very happy. But that wasn't the end of it. Niamh looked at her new husband and told him, "I can't stay here long, Oisín. I have to go back to Tír ná nÓg or I will grow old and die. Will you come with me?"

Oisín didn't hesitate. "Anywhere you go, I go."

He didn't even say goodbye to his family. As far as Fionn MacCumhaill knew, his son had disappeared off the face of the Earth. Which was true in a way because Tír ná nÓg is not part of this world.

And then the poor king's worries came true. His son-in-law did indeed become the king, though he didn't steal the crown, he won it in a race.

One of the stranger things about Tír ná nÓg was that it was ruled by whoever was the fastest person there. To decide this, there was a race every seven years. Until then, Niamh's father had never been beaten.

It was different this time, though. The other runners had barely left the start line when Oisín was already at the finish, which was the throne itself.

Oisín was happy as the king of Tír ná nÓg for many years. He and Niamh never grew old. They had two kids, and they were very happy.

But eventually, Oisín became homesick. He missed Ireland and his family and he wanted to go home.

Niamh didn't want him to go. She said that if he went he wouldn't come back to her ever again. He would grow old and blind and, finally, he would die.

"I'll be fine," Oisin promised.

Niamh shook her head, but she knew he would go whether she wanted him to or not. So she gave him a great white horse and said, "Don't ever step off the horse. Don't even touch the ground of Ireland. If you do, you will grow old and die."

Maybe you are rolling your eyes right now. Are you? I bet you are. You know what happens in myths when someone is told not to do something, don't you? That's right, they go and do it.

Well, maybe Oisín will surprise you. Maybe he will be smart and stay on the horse and go back to Tír ná nÓg and continue living happily with Niamh and their two kids.

The Ireland he returned to was nothing like the one he had left. You know how they say one human year is the same as seven years for a dog? Well, one year in Tír ná nÓg was like a hundred in Ireland. So what had seemed like ten years to Oisín in Tír ná nÓg was a thousand in the real world.

The Ireland he had left had been full of forests and small towns with wooden buildings and maybe a couple of stone castles. The Ireland he came back to was full of churches. Fionn MacCumhaill and even Oisín himself had become myths. They had lived so long ago that people had forgotten that they were even real. One young girl even told the story of how Fionn's son had been stolen away by a fairy from another world.

He traveled to where his father's castle had been, but there was nothing left. At least, that was what he thought. He had just been turning to leave when he saw a stone sticking out of the ground. It was the stone bowl they had washed their hands in when they came in from the fields.

The sight of something he remembered in this strange land, the only thing that remained from his home, filled him with a powerful need to touch it. Forgetting what Niamh said, he got off his horse and bent down to feel the stone.

Between the time his foot touched the ground and when he touched the stone with his finger, a thousand years came over Oisín and he found himself lying on the ground, weak, blind, deaf. Powerless and dying.

Of course he touched the ground. You knew he was going to.

Conclusion

We have reached the end of the book. We hope you enjoyed all the myths. If you look in the acknowledgments and references you will find many more to read.

Maybe one day all the things happening now will become myths, just the way Oisín and his father did. Maybe things we learn about in history books will get exaggerated and changed until the stories say that George Washington sucked his thumb for wisdom, or that Hitler was thrown into the center of the Earth by gods called America, Britain, and Russia and that he rules over Hell.

Maybe there really was a king called Ra who lost his throne to a queen called Isis, but it was so long ago that we will never be able to find the proof. Maybe a boy really did kill a guard dog. Maybe a man called Oisín really left Ireland a long time ago, traveled the whole world, and then came back as an old man.

Maybe all these stories have a kernel of truth, which means that there is a tiny, tiny bit of truth hidden in the middle of all the make-believe.

That said, there doesn't seem to be much truth in Fionn MacCumhaill dressing up as a baby. It makes for a good story, though, which is all we need from myths. They are the greatest stories ever told and the greatest stories to read and enjoy.

Thank you for reading.

Acknowledgments

We mentioned at the start of the book that it is very important to give people credit for their work. This is not just about being honest, it is also so that we can recommend some other great books about myths that you will love.

A lot of the stories in this book come to you directly from the original translations of the very old books where they were discovered. Some of the myths about Egypt, for example, were translated *directly* from the walls of the pyramids!

Because these books are so old, a lot of them are available for free. The best website for all things mythological is Sacred-Texts, which you can find at this link: https://www.sacred-texts.com/index.htm.

The problem with some old books is that they are very difficult to read. The Pyramid Texts, for example, are copied down exactly as they were on the walls of the pyramids. Maybe you have noticed that the paint falls off the walls in your house after a few years. Well, imagine what it would look like after a few thousand years! As a result, the Pyramid Texts are missing a lot of stuff that people have had to fill in, using things they have read on other pyramids, or they have heard from other people.

One excellent writer who was very good at taking these difficult-to-read texts and making them fun is Padraic Colum. His book, *Orpheus: Myths of the World,* is an interesting and fun book that tells stories from all over the world, including Japan and Latin America, and New Zealand—places we didn't get to visit in this book. A lot of his books are also available on the Sacred-Texts website.

Another great writer who has many books about myths and other amazing stories like King Arthur and Robin Hood is Roger Lancelyn Green. If you enjoyed this book, you should definitely read his.

This book owes a lot to many other writers and books. If you want to see a full list of other books you might like, or to know where some of the stories and facts in this book came from, look at the references at the end.

We hope you enjoy all your future journeys through mythology! You have a lifetime of them to come.

Greetings!

As fellow passionate readers of history and mythology we aim to create the very best books for our readers.

We invite you to join our VIP list so that you can be the first to receive new books and exclusives. Plus you will receive a free gift!

Sign Up Today

https://www.subscribepage.com/hba

References

Apollodorus. (1921). *The library*. (J.G. Frazer, Trans.). Loeb Classical Library.

Bellows, H. A. (Trans.). (1936). *The poetic Edda*. Princeton University Press.

Britannica, T. Editors of Encyclopaedia (2017, April 27). *Cú Chulainn*. Encyclopedia Britannica. https://www.britannica.com/topic/Cu-Chulainn

Britannica, T. Editors of Encyclopaedia (2018, December 7). *Lugus*. Encyclopedia Britannica. https://www.britannica.com/topic/Lugus

Budge, W. (1912). *Legends of the gods*. Createspace Independent Publishing Platform.

Bulfinch, T. (1855). *The age of fable, or stories of the gods and heroes*. Sanborn, Carter, and Bazin.

Butler, S. (Trans.). (1898). *The Iliad of Homer*. Longmans, Green, & Co.

Colum, P. (1930). *Orpheus, myths of the world*. Macmillan.

Colum, P. (1920). *The children of Odin: The book of northern myths*. Macmillan.

Cross, T.P. & Slover, C.H. (Eds.). (1936). Bricriu's feast. *Ancient Irish tales* (pp. 254-280). (G. Henderson, Trans.). George G. Harraph & Co.

Curtin, J. (1890). *Myths and folk-lore of Ireland*. (1st American Edition). Little Brown.

Dillon, M. (1998, September 19). *Celtic religion*. Encyclopædia Britannica. https://www.britannica.com/topic/Celtic-religion.

Encyclopædia Britannica, inc. (1998, July 20). *Gaelic revival*. Encyclopædia Britannica. https://www.britannica.com/art/Gaelic-revival.

Encyclopædia Britannica, inc. (2012, March 2). *Irish literary renaissance*. Encyclopædia Britannica. https://www.britannica.com/event/Irish-literary-renaissance.

Encyclopædia Britannica, inc. (2020, November 26). *Viking*. Encyclopædia Britannica. https://www.britannica.com/topic/Viking-people.

Fry, S. (2017). *Mythos: A retelling of the myths of Ancient Greece*. Michael Joseph.

Gregory, Lady A. (1902). *Cuchulain of Muirthemne*. Alfred Nutt.

Gregory, Lady A. (1904). *Gods and fighting men: the story of the Tuatha de Danaan and of the Fianna of Ireland*. J. Murray.

Hesiod. (1936). *Hesiod. The Homeric hymns and Homerica*. (H. G. Evelyn-White, Trans.). (3rd rev. ed.). Loeb Classical Library.

Hornblower, S. (1999, July 26). *Alexander the Great*. Encyclopædia Britannica.

https://www.britannica.com/place/ancient-Greece/Alexander-the-Great.

Jacobs, J., & Batten, J.D. (1968). *Celtic fairy tales*. Dover Publications.

Jordan, M. (1993). *Myths of the world*. Kyle Cathie.

Mercer, S. (Trans.). (1952). *The pyramid texts*. Longsmans, Green Co.

Meyer, K. (1904). The boyish exploits of Finn. *Eriu*, 1, 180-190. Royal Irish Academy. (Original work published 1881). http://www.jstor.org/stable/30007946.

Monaghan, P. (2004). *Encyclopedia of Celtic mythology and folklore*. (2nd ed.). Facts on File.

Morford, M., Lenardon, R. J., & Sham, M. (2019). *Myth summary chapter 8: Athena*. Oxford University Press. https://global.oup.com/us/companion.websites/9780199997329/student/materials/chapter8/summary/.

Murray, M.A. (1920). *Ancient Egyptian legends*. John Murray.

National Geographic Society. (2019, January 15). *Alexander the Great*. National Geographic Society. https://www.nationalgeographic.org/encyclopedia/alexander-great/.

Ovid. (2009). *Metamorphoses*. (A.D. Melville, Trans.). (Oxford World's Classics). Oxford University Press.

Persephone. Greek Mythology Wiki. (2009, May 17). https://greekmythology.wikia.org/wiki/Persephone.

Rank, O. (1914). *The myth of the birth of the hero.* (E. Robbins & S. Jelliffe, Trans.). (1st ed. in English). The Journal of Nervous and Mental Disease. (Original work published 1909).

Roman, M. & Roman, L. (2010). *Encyclopedia of Greek and Roman mythology.* Facts on File.

Sheppard, Norman. (2008, September 22). *Tyr.* The Norse Gods. https://thenorsegods.com/tyr/.

Sturluson, S. (1960). *The prose Edda.* (A. Brodeur, Trans.). American-Scandinavian Foundation. (Original work published 1916).

Turville-Petre, E. O. G. (1999, July 26). *Germanic religion and mythology.* Encyclopædia Britannica. https://www.britannica.com/topic/Germanic-religion-and-mythology.

Yeats, W.B. (1893). *The Celtic twilight.* Lawrence and Bullen.